YOU
are a
BAD
ASS

HOW TO STOP DOUBTING *Your Greatness*

AND START LIVING AN *Awesome life*

Jen Sincero

JOHN
MURRAY
LEARNING

First published in United States of America in 2013 by Running Press,
a member of the Perseus Books Group.

This edition published in Great Britain in 2016 by John Murray Learning, an imprint of
Hodder and Stoughton. An Hachette UK company.

Copyright © 2013 Jen Sincero

The right of Jen Sincero to be identified as the Author
of the Work has been asserted by her in accordance with
the Copyright, Designs and Patents Act 1988.

Database right Hodder & Stoughton (makers)

British Library Cataloguing in Publication Data: a catalogue record
for this title is available from the British Library.

Paperback: 9781473649521
eBook: 9781473649491

1

The publisher has used its best endeavours to ensure that any website addresses referred to in
this book are correct and active at the time of going to press. However, the publisher and
the author have no responsibility for the websites and can make no guarantee that a site will
remain live or that the content will remain relevant, decent or appropriate.

The publisher has made every effort to mark as such all words which it believes to be
trademarks. The publisher should also like to make it clear that the presence of a word in the
book, whether marked or unmarked, in no way affects its legal status as a trademark.

Every reasonable effort has been made by the publisher to trace the copyright holders of
material in this book. Any errors or omissions should be notified in writing to the publisher,
who will endeavour to rectify the situation for any reprints and future editions.

Printed and bound in Great Britain by Clays Ltd, St Ives plc.

John Murray Learning policy is to use papers that are natural, renewable
and recyclable products and made from wood grown in sustainable forests.
The logging and manufacturing processes are expected to conform to
the environmental regulations of the country of origin.

Carmelite House
50 Victoria Embankment
London EC4Y 0DZ

www.hodder.co.uk

For my unfailingly sweet and supportive Dad and brother Stephen

CONTENTS

INTRODUCTION   10

PART 1:
HOW YOU GOT THIS WAY

CHAPTER 1: My Subconscious Made Me Do It   18

CHAPTER 2: The G-Word   28

CHAPTER 3: Present as a Pigeon   35

CHAPTER 4: The Big Snooze   41

CHAPTER 5: Self-Perception Is a Zoo   48

PART 2:
HOW TO EMBRACE YOUR INNER BADASS

CHAPTER 6: Love the One You Is   52

CHAPTER 7: I Know You Are But What Am I?   63

CHAPTER 8: What Are You Doing Here?   71

CHAPTER 9: Loincloth Man   81

PART 3:
HOW TO TAP INTO THE MOTHERLODE

CHAPTER 10: Meditation 101   85

CHAPTER 11: Your Brain Is Your Bitch   92

CHAPTER 12: Lead with Your Crotch   101

CHAPTER 13: Give and Let Give   109

CHAPTER 14: Gratitude: The Gateway Drug
              to Awesomeness   113

CHAPTER 15: Forgive or Fester   121

CHAPTER 16: Loosen Your Bone, Wilma   129

PART 4:
HOW TO GET OVER YOUR B.S. ALREADY

CHAPTER 17: It's So Easy Once You Figure
              Out It Isn't Hard   135

CHAPTER 18: Procrastination, Perfection,
              and a Polish Beer Garden   149

CHAPTER 19: The Drama of Overwhelm   156

CHAPTER 20: Fear Is for Suckers   166

CHAPTER 21: Millions of Mirrors   176

CHAPTER 22: The Sweet Life   188

PART 5:
HOW TO KICK SOME ASS

CHAPTER 23: The Almighty Decision   191

CHAPTER 24: Money, Your New Best Friend   201

CHAPTER 25: Remember to Surrender   224

CHAPTER 26: Doing vs. Spewing   230

CHAPTER 27: Beam Me Up, Scotty   242

RESOURCES   245

ACKNOWLEDGMENTS   254

INTRODUCTION

You can start out with nothing, and out of nothing, and out of no way, a way will be made.
—**Reverend Michael Bernard Beckwith; former drug enthusiast turned spiritual enthusiast turned inspirational badass**

I used to think quotes like this were a bunch of crap. I also didn't understand what the hell they were talking about. I mean, not that I cared. I was too cool. What little I knew about the self-help/spiritual world I found to be unforgivably cheesy: it reeked of desperation, rah-rah churchiness and unwanted hugs from unappealing strangers. And don't even get me started on how grouchy I used to be about God.

At the same time, there was all this stuff about my life that I desperately wanted to change and, had I been able to bulldoze through my holier-than-thouism, I could have really used some help around here. I mean, overall I was doing pretty well—I'd published a couple of books, had lots of great friends, a close family, an apartment, a car that ran, food, teeth, clothes, clean drinking water—compared to the majority of the planet, my life was a total cream puff. But compared to what I knew I was capable of, I was, shall we say, unimpressed.

I always felt like, *Come ON, this is the best I can do? Really? I'm going to make just enough to pay my rent this month? Again? And I'm going to spend another year dating a bunch of weirdos so I can be in all these wobbly, non-committal relationships and create even more drama? Really? And am I seriously going to question what my deeper purpose is and wallow in the misery of that quagmire for the millionth time?*

It. Was. A. Snore.

I felt like I was going through the motions of living my lukewarm life with the occasional flare-ups of awesomeness here and there. And the most painful part was that deep down I KNEW I was a total rock star, that I had the power to give and receive and love with the best of 'em, that I could leap tall buildings in a single bound and could create anything I put my mind to and . . . *What's that? I just got a parking ticket? You have got to be kidding me, let me see that. I can't afford to pay this, it's like my third one this month! I'm going down there to talk to them right now . . .* then, doop de do, off I'd go, consumed once again by low-level minutiae, only to find myself, a few weeks later, wondering where those few weeks went and how it could possibly be that I was still stuck in my rickety-ass apartment, eating dollar tacos by myself every night.

I'm assuming if you're reading this that there are some areas of your life that aren't looking so good either. And that you know could be looking a whole lot better. Maybe you're living with your soul mate and are joyfully sharing your gifts with the world, but are so broke that your dog is on his own if he wants to get fed. Maybe you're doing great financially and you have a deep connection to your higher purpose, but you can't remember the last time you wet your pants laughing. Or maybe you suck equally at all of the above and spend your free time crying. Or drinking. Or getting pissed off at all the meter maids who have precision timing and no sense of humor who, in your mind, are partly responsible for your personal financial crisis. Or maybe you have everything you've ever wanted but for some reason you still feel unfulfilled.

This isn't necessarily about making millions of dollars or helping solve the world's problems or getting your own TV show, unless that's your thing. Your calling could simply be to take care of your family or to grow the perfect tulip.

This is about getting mighty clear about what makes you happy and what makes you feel the most alive, and then creating it instead of pretending you can't have it. Or that you don't deserve it. Or that you're a greedy egomaniacal fathead for wanting more than you already have. Or listening to what Dad and Aunt Mary think you *should* be doing.

It's about having the cojones to show up as the brightest, happiest, badassiest version of yourself, whatever that looks like to you.

The good news is that in order to do this, all you need to do is make one simple shift:

You need to go from **wanting** to change your life to **deciding** to change your life.

· ·

Wanting can be done sitting on the couch with a bong in your hand and a travel magazine in your lap.

Deciding means jumping in all the way, doing whatever it takes, and going after your dreams with the tenacity of a dateless cheerleader a week before prom night.

· ·

You'll probably have to do things you never imagined you'd do because if any of your friends saw you doing it, or spending money on it, you'd never live it down. Or they'd be concerned about you. Or they'd stop being friends with you because now you're all weird and different. You'll have to believe in things you can't see as well as some things that you have full-on proof are impossible. You're gonna have to push past your fears, fail over and over again and make a habit of doing things you're not so comfy doing. You're going to have to let go of old, limiting beliefs and cling to your decision to create the life you desire like your life depends on it.

Because guess what? Your life does depend on it.

As challenging as this may sound, it's nowhere near as brutal as waking up in the middle of the night feeling like someone parked a car on your chest, crushed under the realization that your life is zooming by and you have yet to start living it in a way that has any real meaning to you.

You may have heard stories about people who had these major breakthroughs when the shit really hit the fan—they found a lump or got their electricity turned off or were moments away from having sex with strangers to buy drugs when suddenly they woke up, transformed. But you don't have to wait until you hit rock bottom to start crawling out of your hole. All you have to do is make the decision. And you can make it right now.

There's a great line from the poet Anaïs Nin that reads: "And the day came when the risk to remain tight in a bud was more painful than the risk it took to blossom." This is how it was for me, and how I think it is for most people. My journey was a process (and still is) that started with my *decision* to make some serious changes, regardless of what I had to do to make them. None of the things I'd already tried were working: mulling it over and over with my equally broke friends and my therapist, working my ass off, going out for a beer and hoping it would take care of itself . . . I was at the point where I would try anything to get my act together, and Lawdy Lawd Lawd Lawd, it's like the Universe was testing me to see just how serious I was.

I went to motivational seminars where they made me wear a name tag and high-five the person next to me while shouting, "You're awesome and so am I!" I beat a pillow with a baseball bat and shrieked like I was on fire, I bonded with my spirit guide, participated in a group ceremony where I married myself, wrote a love letter to my uterus, read every self-help book under the sun, and spent blood-curdling amounts of money I did not have hiring private coaches.

Basically, I took one for the team.

If you're new to the self-help world, I'm hoping this book will ease you into some of the basic concepts that totally changed my life so you can have a breakthrough, too, without making you want to run off screaming in the process. If you've already dipped your toe in the self-help pond, I hope it will say something in a new way that turns a light on so you can make some major shifts, create some tangible results, and someday wake up crying tears of giddy disbelief that you get to be you.

And if I can save one person from ever having to take their inner child on a play date, I have done my job.

My main focus when I started working on myself was how to make money. I had no idea how to make it on a consistent basis, and was totally weirded out by admitting that I even wanted to in the first place. I was a writer and a musician; I felt it was sufficient—and quite noble thank you very much—to focus on my art and let the money part work itself out. THAT went real well! But I saw so many people doing such sleazy and heartbreaking things to make money, not to mention those people who were working jobs that were death-of-a-thousand-wounds boring, that I wanted no part of it. Add to that my slew of other crippling beliefs about the unholy dollar and it's a wonder I wasn't eating out of a dumpster.

I finally realized that I needed not only to focus on making money, but that I also needed to get over my fear and loathing of it if I wanted to start pulling it in. This is when the self-help books started infiltrating my house, and the name tags assumed their mandatory and humiliating post above my left boob. Eventually I took my credit card debt to unthinkable heights by forking over more money than I'd paid for all my janky cars put together and hired my first coach. Within the first six months, I tripled my income with an online business that I created around coaching writers. And now I've grown it to a place where it affords me the means and the luxury to travel the world freely, while I write, speak, play music, and coach people in all areas of their lives, using many of the concepts I used to so enjoy rolling my eyes at and with which I am now obsessed.

In an attempt to help you get to where you want to go too, I'm going to ask you to roll with some pretty out-there things throughout this book, and I want to encourage you to have an open mind. No, on second thought, I want to yell in your face about it: STAY OPEN OR ELSE YOU ARE SCREWED. I mean it. This is really important. You've gotten to where you are right now by doing whatever it is you're doing, so if you're less than impressed with your current situation, you clearly need to change things up.

••

If you want to live a life you've never lived, you have to do things you've never done.

••

I don't care how big a loser you may or may not perceive yourself to be right now, the fact that you're literate, have the luxury of time to read this book and the money to buy it puts you way ahead of the game.

This isn't something to feel guilty or whiney or superior about. But it is something to appreciate, and should you make the decision to really go for it, know that you are extremely well-poised to knock it out of the park and share your awesomeness with the world. Because that's really what this is all about.

We need smart people with huge hearts and creative minds to manifest all the wealth, resources, and support they need to make their difference in the world.

We need people to feel happy and fulfilled and loved so they don't take their shit out on themselves and other people and the planet and our animal friends.

We need to be surrounded by people who radiate self-love and abundance so we don't program future generations with gnarly beliefs like *money is bad* and *I'm not good-enough* and *I can't live the way I want to live*.

We need kickass people to be out of struggle and living large and on purpose so they can be an inspiration to others who want to rise up, too.

The first thing I'm going to ask you to do is to believe that we live in a world of limitless possibilities. I don't care if you have a lifetime of proof that you can't stop shoving food in your face or that people are intrinsically evil or that you couldn't keep a man if you were hand-cuffed to his ankles—believe that anything is possible anyway.

See what happens—what do you have to lose? If you try getting through this book and decide it's a bunch of crap, you can go back to your sucky life. But maybe, if you put your disbelief aside, roll up your sleeves, take some risks, and totally go for it, you'll wake up one day and realize you're living the kind of life you used to be jealous of.

PART 1:
HOW YOU GOT THIS WAY

CHAPTER 1:

MY SUBCONSCIOUS
MADE ME DO IT

You are a victim of the rules you live by.
—**Jenny Holzer; artist, thinker, blurter of brilliance**

Many years ago I was in a terrible bowling accident. My friends and I were at the tail end of a heated tiebreaker, and I was so focused on making a great show of my final shot—leaping into action, loudly declaring my impending victory, dancing and twirling my way through my approach—that I didn't realize where my feet were when I let go of the ball.

This was the moment I was to learn how serious the bowling

community is about penalizing those who roll with one toe over the line. They pour oil or wax or lube or something unimaginably slippery all over the alley, and should someone accidentally slide out of bounds while attempting the perfect hook shot, she will find her feet flying out from under her and her ass crashing down onto a surface that even an airborne bowling ball can't crack.

A few weeks later whilst lolling about in bed with this guy I met at Macy's, I explained that ever since my accident, I'm now woken up in the middle of the night with excruciating pain in my feet. According to my acupuncturist, this is from the nerves in my back getting slammed when I fell, and in order to sleep through the night I'd need a new, firmer mattress.

"I have pains in my feet when I sleep too!" He said, raising himself up for an unreciprocated high five.

It's not just because I'm not into the whole high-five thing that I left him hanging, but also because I was annoyed with him. I already find mattress shopping to be totally bizarre and embarrassing—lying on your side with a pillow between your thighs for all to see like it's anyone's business—but the fact that I had to do it with my salesman lying next to me, begging for a high-fiver, was more than I could handle.

I couldn't help but notice that all the other salesmen simply stood at the end of the bed, rattling off mattress facts while their clients tested out a myriad of positions, but not mine. He'd lower down next to me on his back, arms crossed over his chest, and thoughtfully chat away, staring at the ceiling like we were at summer camp. I mean, he was nice enough and incredibly knowledgeable about coils and latex and memory foam, but I was scared to roll over for fear he'd start spooning me.

Was I too friendly? Should I not have asked him where he was from? Did he think I meant something else when I patted the empty space next to me to test the pillow top?

I obviously should have asked Freak Show Bob to get off the damn
bed, or found someone else to help me, instead of sneaking out the
door and blowing my only opportunity that week to go mattress shopping, but I didn't want to embarrass him.

I didn't want to embarrass *him*!

This is pretty much how my family was trained to deal with any
sort of potentially uncomfortable interaction. Along with the fail-safe
method of running in the opposite direction, other tools in our confrontation toolbox also included: freeze, talk about the weather, go
blank, and burst into tears the moment you're out of earshot.

Our lack of confrontation-management skills was no great surprise
considering the fact that my mother comes from a long lineage of
WASPs. Her parents were the types who believed that children were
to be seen and not heard, and who looked upon any sort of emotional
display with the same, horrified disdain usually reserved for cheap
scotch and non–Ivy League educations.

And even though my mother went on to create a household for us
that was as warm, loving, and laughter-filled as they come, it took
years for me to finally learn how to form a sentence when presented
with the blood-chilling phrase, "We need to talk."

All this is to say that it's not your fault that you're fucked up. It's
your fault if you *stay* fucked up, but the foundation of your
fuckedupedness is something that's been passed down through generations of your family, like a coat of arms or a killer cornbread recipe,
or in my case, equating confrontation with heart failure.

When you came screaming onto this planet you were truly a bun-
dle of joy, a wide-eyed creature incapable of doing anything but being
in the moment. You had no idea that you had a body, let alone that you
should be ashamed of it. When you looked around, everything just *was*.
There was nothing about your world that was scary or too expensive
or so last year as far as you were concerned. If something came near

your mouth, you stuck it in, if it came near your hand, you grabbed it. You were simply a human . . . *being*.

While you explored and expanded into your new world, you also received messages from the people around you about the way things are. From the moment you could take it in, they started filling you up with a lifetime's worth of beliefs, many of which have nothing to do with who you actually are or what is necessarily true (e.g. the world is a dangerous place, you're too fat, homosexuality is a curse, size matters, hair shouldn't grow there, going to college is important, being a musician or an artist isn't a real career, etc.).

The main source of this information was, of course, your parents, assisted by society at large. When they were raising you, your parents, in a genuine effort to protect you and educate you and love you with all their hearts (hopefully), passed on the beliefs they learned from their parents, who learned them from their parents, who learned them from their parents. . . .

The trouble is, many of these beliefs have nothing to do with who *they* actually are/were or what is actually true.

I realize I'm making it sound like we're all crazy, but that's because we kind of are.

••

Most people are living in an illusion based on someone else's beliefs.

••

Until they wake up. Which is what this book will hopefully help you do.

Here's how it works: We as humans have a conscious mind and a subconscious mind. Most of us are only aware of our conscious minds, however, because that's where we process all our information. It's where we figure things out, judge, obsess, analyze, criticize, worry that our ears are too big, decide once and for all to stop eating fried food, grasp that $2 + 2 = 4$, try to remember where the hell we left the car keys, etc.

The conscious mind is like a relentless overachiever, incessantly spinning around from thought to thought, stopping only when we sleep, and then starting up again the second we open our eyes. Our conscious mind, otherwise known as our frontal lobe, doesn't fully develop until sometime around puberty.

Our subconscious mind, on the other hand, is the non-analytical part of our brain that's fully developed the moment we arrive here on earth. It's all about feelings and instincts and erupting into ear-piercing temper tantrums in the middle of supermarkets. It's also where we store all the early, outside information we get.

The subconscious mind believes everything because it has no filter, it doesn't know the difference between what's true and what's not true. If our parents tell us that nobody in our family knows how to make money, we believe them. If they show us that marriage means punching each other in the face, we believe them. We believe them when they tell us that some fat guy in a red suit is going to climb down the chimney and bring us presents—why wouldn't we believe any of the other garbage they feed us?

Our subconscious mind is like a little kid who doesn't know any better and, not coincidentally, receives most of its information when we're little kids and don't know any better (because our frontal lobes, the conscious part of our brains, hasn't fully formed yet). We take in information via the words, smiles, frowns, heavy sighs, raised eyebrows, tears, laughter, etc., of the people surrounding us with zero ability to filter any of it, and it all gets lodged in our squishy little subconscious minds as the "truth" (otherwise known as our "beliefs") where it lives, undisturbed and unanalyzed, until we're on the therapy couch decades later or checking ourselves into rehab, again.

I can pretty much guarantee that every time you tearfully ask your-self the question, "WTF is my problem?!" the answer lies in some lame, limiting, and false subconscious belief that you've been dragging around without even realizing it. Which means that understanding this is majorly important. So let's review, shall we?

1) Our subconscious mind contains the blueprint for our lives. It's running the show based on the unfiltered information it gathered when we were kids, otherwise known as our "beliefs."

2) We are, for the most part, completely oblivious to these sub-conscious beliefs that run our lives.

3) When our conscious minds finally develop and show up for work, no matter how big and smart and highfalutin they grow to be, they're still being controlled by the beliefs we're carrying around in our subconscious minds.

••

Our conscious mind thinks it's in control, but it isn't.

Our subconscious mind doesn't think about any-thing, but *is* in control.

••

This is why so many of us stumble through life doing everything we know in our conscious minds to do, yet remain mystified by what's keeping us from creating the excellent lives we want.

For example, let's say you were raised by a father who was constantly struggling financially, who walked around kicking the furniture and grumbling about how money doesn't grow on trees, and who neglected you because he was always off trying, and for the most part failing, to make a living. Your subconscious took this in *at face value* and might have developed beliefs such as:

- Money = struggle

- Money is unavailable.

- It's money's fault that I was abandoned by my father.

- Money sucks and causes pain.

Cut to you as an adult who, in your conscious mind, would love nothing more than to be raking in the dough, but who is subconsciously mistrusting of money, believes it's unavailable to you and who worries that if you make it, you'll be abandoned by someone you love. You may then manifest these subconscious beliefs by staying broke no matter how hard you *consciously* try to make money, or by repeatedly making tons of money and then losing it in order to avoid being abandoned, or in a plethora of other, frustrating ways.

••

No matter what you say you want, if you've got an underlying subconscious belief that it's going to cause you pain or isn't available to you, you either A) Won't let yourself have it, or B) You will let yourself have it, but you'll be rill fucked up about it. And then you'll go off and lose it anyway.

••

We don't realize that by eating that fourth doughnut or by ignoring our intuition and marrying that guy who's an awful lot like our low-down, cheatin' daddy, that we're being driven by our subconscious minds, not our conscious minds. And that when our subconscious beliefs are out of alignment with the things and experiences we want in our conscious minds (and hearts), it creates confusing conflicts between what we're trying to create and what we're actually creating. It's like we're driving with one foot on the gas and one foot on the brake. (Obviously we all have awesome subconscious beliefs as well, but we're not talking about those right now.)

Here are some other scenarios that may or may not ring a bell:

Conscious Mind: I long to find and marry my soul mate.
Subconscious Mind: Intimacy leads to pain and suffering.
Finger: Ringless

Conscious Mind: I want to lose 25 pounds.
Subconscious Mind: People aren't safe; I must build a shield to protect myself.
Body: A fortress of flab

Conscious Mind: I'm hot and sexy and want to get it on.
Subconscious Mind: Physical pleasure is shameful.
Sex Life: Yawn

Conscious Mind: I want to travel the world.
Subconscious Mind: Fun = irresponsible = I won't be loved
Passport: Blank

It's sort of like not being able to enjoy sitting on your front porch anymore because it totally reeks of something foul out there. You can come up with all these brilliant ways to deal with the problem—light incense, set up fans, blame it on the dog—but until you realize that something has crawled under your house and died, your problems will linger on, stinking up your life.

The first key to ridding yourself of limiting subconscious beliefs is to become aware of them. Because until you're aware of what's really going on, you'll keep working with your conscious mind (think you need to paint the porch) to solve a problem that's buried far beneath it (dead skunk removal) in your subconscious, which is an exercise in futility.

Take a minute to look at some of the less-than-impressive areas of your life and think about the underlying beliefs that could have created them. Let's take the old crowd-pleaser, lack of money, for example. Are you making far less money than you know you're capable of earning? Have you reached a certain income level that, no matter what you do, you can't seem to go above? Does generating an abundance of money consistently seem like something you're not even physically capable of? If so, write down the first five things that come to your mind when you think about money. Is your list full of hope and bravado or fear and loathing? What are your parents' beliefs about money? What are the beliefs of the other people you grew up around?

What was their relationship with money like? Do you see any connection between their money beliefs and yours?

Later on in this book I'm going to give you tools to go much deeper with your subconscious beliefs and fix whatever's blocking you from living the kind of life you'd love to live, but for now, practice stepping aside, notice what's happening in the dysfunctional areas of your life and strengthen your almighty awareness muscle. Start waking up to the stories you're working with in your subconscious (I'll have to do things I hate in order to make money, I'll feel trapped if I get into an intimate relationship, if I go on a diet I'll never get to eat anything fun again, if I enjoy sex I'll burn in Hell with the rest of the dirty sinners, etc.). Because once you see what's really going on, you can start to drag out the stinky carcasses of your limiting subconscious beliefs and give them the heave-ho, thereby opening up the space to invite the fresh, new, awesome beliefs and experiences that you'd love to have, into your life.

CHAPTER 2:

THE G WORD

If you want to find the secrets of the universe,
think in terms of energy, frequency and vibration.
—Nokola Tesla; inventor, physicist, supergenius

When I lived in Albuquerque, New Mexico, my friends and I used to hang out at this western bar called Midnight Rodeo. It was the kind of place that had curling irons and hair spray in the women's bathroom, Bud Light on permanent special for two bucks a can, and a solid oak dance floor the size of a cornfield.

We were all from the East Coast and were way too cool for country music, so at first we'd go just to snootily make fun of it all, taking great pride in being the first to spot a particularly gigantic belt buckle or a cowboy sporting one of them handlebar mustaches big enough to cover five upper lips. But our favorite part was the line dancing. We'd stare mesmerized by the giant, choreographed mass of Garth Brooks fans, stomping around in synchronized woo-hooery with their thumbs purposefully tucked into the front pockets of their jeans.

It was so hilarious that we started joining in ourselves, waving from the middle of the sea of cowboy hats to our friends—*watch this!* Then, uh, we'd stay on the floor for the next song, just to try and get that part down where you click your heels right before the spin. Then we found ourselves sneaking off every weekend to merrily line dance our little achy breaky hearts out.

This is sort of the same way the God thing happened for me. It started out with much snarkiness and eye rolling, but I was so broke and clueless and sick of being such a weenie about really going for it in my life, that I was open for suggestions. Which is why, when I started reading books on finding your calling and making money and getting over yourself already, and they all had this spiritual side to them, I didn't toss them in the Goodwill pile with my usual *this God/spirituality crap is for suckers* attitude. Instead I decided to give good old God a chance because I had nothing to lose. Literally. And lo and behold, some of it wasn't totally idiotic. So I started reading more about it. Then I started studying it. Then I started putting it into practice. Then I noticed how much better it made me feel. Then I started believing it. Then I noticed all these awesome shifts starting to happen in my life. Then I became obsessed with it. Then I started loving it. Then I started radically changing my life with it. Then I started teaching it. Now I'm basically riding the mechanical bull about it, punching my fist in the air and hollering to the guy manning the controls, "Hit it, Wayne!"

Wherever you happen to stand on the God issue, let me just say that that this whole improving your life thing is going to be a lot eas-

ier if you have an open mind about it. Call it whatever you want—
God, Goddess, The Big Guy, The Universe, Source Energy, Higher
Power, The Grand Poobah, gut, intuition, Spirit, The Force, The Zone,
The Lord, The Vortex, The Mother Lode—it doesn't matter. Personally,
I find the God word to be a tad too loaded, I prefer Source Energy,
The Universe, The Vortex, Spirit, The Mother Lode (all of which I will
use interchangeably throughout this book, FYI). Whatever you choose
to call it isn't important, what is important is that you start to develop
an awareness of, and a relationship with, the Source Energy that's surrounding you and within you (which is all the same energy), and
which will be your best pal ever if you give it a chance. Because here's
the thing:

All of us are connected to this limitless power and
most of us aren't using but a fraction of it.

Our energy is taking a joy ride in these bodies of ours; learning,
growing, and evolving along the way (one would hope, anyway—I
suppose, numbing, shrinking and moving back in with our parents is
also an option), until our corporal journey comes to an end and we
move on . . . *thanks for the lift!* This realization, that we're made up of,
and connected to, Source Energy, made me want to have a deeper
understanding of spirituality so I could make my physical experience
as awesome as possible. And let me tell you, ever since I got into it, it
has been awesomeness maximus.

When I'm connected with Source Energy and in the flow, I am so
much more powerful, so much more in tune to my physical world and
the world beyond, and just so much happier in general. And the more
I meditate and the more attention I give to this relationship with my

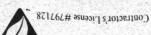

invisible superpower, the more effortlessly I can manifest the things I want into my life, and do it with such specificity and at such a rapid rate that it makes my hair stand up. It's like I've finally figured out how to make my magic wand work.

If loving Spirit is wrong, I don't wanna be right.

HERE IS THE FOUNDATION FOR ALL THE WORK WE'RE ABOUT TO DO TOGETHER ON YOUR LIFE:

- The Universe is made up of Source Energy.

- All energy vibrates at a certain frequency. Which means you're vibrating at a certain frequency, and everything you desire, and don't desire, is also vibrating at a certain frequency.

- Vibration attracts like vibration.

Otherwise known as The Law of Attraction, the basic idea is: Focus on that which makes you feel good and ye shall find (attract) that which makes you feel good.

We're all attracting energy to ourselves all the time whether we realize it or not. And when we're vibrating at a low frequency (feeling pessimistic, needy, victimized, jealous, shameful, worried, convinced we are ugly) yet expect high frequency, awesome things and experiences to come into our lives, we are often disappointed.

You need to raise your frequency to match the vibration of the one you want to tune into.

It's like trying to listen to a certain radio station but tuning in at the wrong frequency. If you have a hot and sexy date and want to listen to 105.9FM Slow Jamz, but set your dial to 89.9FM National Public Radio, you're not only going to be Slow Jamless, but you're more likely to attract a discussion about immigration laws in the U.S. instead of attracting a relaxed and candlelit body that's in the mood for love.

•••

The Universe will match whatever vibration you put out. And you can't fool The Universe.

•••

Which is why when you're vibrating at a high frequency, awesome things seem to flow to you effortlessly and you seem to stumble over the perfect people and opportunities all the time (and vice versa). As Albert Einstein observed, "Coincidence is God's way of remaining anonymous."

When you learn to consciously master the energetic realm, believe in the not yet seen, and stay in your highest frequency, you harness your innate power to create the reality you desire.

So once again, good ole awareness is your key to freedom. Once you realize that you can dramatically improve your situation by connecting with Source Energy and raising your frequency, you can freakin' do it already (I'll show you exactly how later) instead of opting to stay in the suckhole and feeling like a victim of pathetic circumstances such as microwaving ramen in its Styrofoam cup for dinner or working for someone who makes your flesh crawl.

••

In order to truly raise your vibration, you've got to believe that everything you want is available to you. And the best way to keep this belief strong is by staying connected to Source Energy.

••

It's like we're surrounded by this big, all-you-can-eat buffet of incredible experiences and insights and feelings and opportunities and things and people and ways to share our gifts with the world, and all we have to do is align our energy with what we want and take decisive action to allow this good into our lives. And this decisive action part is key. Sadly, we can't just float around our neighbor's pool on a raft with cup-holders, sipping cocktails and being all high frequency while waiting for unicorns to fly down from the sky. We have to take action—hell-bent-for-glory kind of action.

The trick is to have both parts—energy and action—working in unison: unless your energy is lined up properly with that which you desire, really desire, any action you take is going to require way more effort to get you where you want to go, if it gets you there at all. Once in a while you may get lucky doing one without the other, but if you get very clear on what you truly want (rather than what you think you should want), believe that it's available to you regardless of your present circumstances by staying connected to Source Energy and keeping your frequency high, and take decisive action, you will eventually succeed.

Have you ever had a dream where you're flying and you're having such a blast but then you realize, *hey, wait a minute, I'm flying—I can't fly,* and then you come crashing back down to the ground and you can't get yourself back up again? No matter what you try? This is the way beliefs work. Even if it seems impossible, you have to have faith anyway, and the second you stop believing, you pop the bubble and stop attracting the magic in your life.

The Force is with you.

This isn't just about believing and being all high-vibe when the sun is out and the bunnies are hopping around, either. This is about believing, even when things are at their most uncertain or absolute crappiest, that there is a bright shiny flipside within your reach.

As French author and fearless truth-seeker, André Gide, so aptly put it, "One does not discover new lands without consenting to lose sight of the shore for a very long time." This is about believing that we live in a loving, kind and abundant Universe instead of one that's petty, mean, and likes other people more than it likes you.

This is about your faith being greater than your fear.

CHAPTER 3:

PRESENT AS A PIGEON

If you are depressed, you are living in the past. If you are anxious, you are living in the future. If you are at peace, you are living in the present.

—Lao Tzu; ancient Chinese philosopher, founder of Taoism, could have been one guy or a mythical compilation of many, nobody really knows for sure

I was in yoga class one day and the instructor told us all to get into Pigeon Pose, which is this pose where you stretch one leg out behind you, fold the other one out sideways in front of you and then bend forward and lie down on top of the whole thing. It's fine if you're a pigeon, but it's one of the poses I dread most because my hips don't move that way, it hurts and I'm always scared I'm gonna get stuck.

But even though my body has requested otherwise, I'm in class and going for it, and am determined to "relax into it" even though I'm really just silently begging the dude to tell us to change into a different pose, which he doesn't do because he's too busy talking. He's blabbing on and on and on about our connection to The Universe and our breath and the path to true enlightenment and *holy fucking shit dude will you hurry up I think I'm going to rip something I really do oh my God I think I'm actually stuck how am I going to get out of this pose he's gonna have to come over here and lift me out of it because I really truly am stuck* and then whoosh . . .

I breathe into it. I shut off the relentless yammering in my brain, get quiet, and surrender. I feel my body shift and go deeper into the pose than it's ever gone before. The pain is gone. The panic is gone. I am one with The Universe. But then I realize that I really do think I'm stuck and *seriously what the hell dude are you going to talk all night we've been in this freakin' pose for five minutes for real and by the way my knee just got all hot and you really are not going to shut up even though I keep thinking you finally are but then you keep going* and then, whoosh . . .

I reconnect. I'm back in The Zone. I melt deeply into this pose and feel such bliss and true connection to something much larger than myself.

This flip-flopping between freaking out in our heads and "breathing into the Now" is basically how most of us go through life. Instead of worrying about the possibility of dislocating a hip (the future) or about how bad I was at this pose (the past), I could have luxuriated in the magnificence available to me in the moment.

It never ceases to amaze me the precious time we spend chasing the squirrels around our brains, playing out our dramas, worrying about unwanted facial hair, seeking adoration, justifying our actions, complaining about slow Internet connections, dissecting the lives of idiots, when we are sitting in the middle of a full-blown miracle that is happening right here, right now.

We're on a planet that somehow knows how to rotate on its axis and follow a defined path while it hurtles through space! Our hearts beat! We can see! We have love, laughter, language, living rooms, computers, compassion, cars, fire, fingernails, flowers, music, medicine, mountains, muffins! We live in a limitless Universe overflowing with miracles! The fact that we aren't stumbling around in an inconsolable state of sobbing awe is appalling. The Universe must be like, *what more do I have to do to wake these bitches up? Make water, their most precious resource, rain down from the sky?*

The Universe loves us so much, and wants us to partake in the miraculous so badly, that sometimes she delivers little wake-up calls. Like in the movies when someone narrowly escapes death and is so overjoyed and grateful that they take to the streets, skipping and laughing and madly hugging everyone in sight. Suddenly all their "problems" fall away and the miracle of being alive, today, in this moment takes over the screen. I know someone who got sucked through a dam and almost died who now speaks about it as one of his most profound and life-changing experiences. Not that I'd wish that on anyone, but take heart in the fact that should you require some sort of catastrophe for your transformation, it can be cosmically arranged.

The Universe has also surrounded us with the perfect teachers. Animals, for example. Animals are in the present all the time, and their secret power is to pull us in with them. My friend's dog is so happy to see her every single time she walks in the door it's like she's about to free him from forty years of imprisonment. Even if she's only been gone for an hour. You're here. I'm here. I love you. I'm gonna pee all over the floor about it.

Little kids are also excellent guides. Kids get so wrapped up in the joy of drawing or pretending or discovering that they'd rarely eat or bathe or sleep if we didn't make them. They are constantly creating in a state of free-flowing, concentrated bliss, they haven't yet learned to worry about what other people think of them or that perhaps they're not as talented at finger painting as Lucy next door is. They are in the moment. There is fun in the moment. End of story.

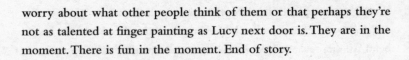

We would be wise to take more of our cues from the beasts and babies.

All the stuff we're so worried about creating and fixated on becoming is already right here, right now. The money you want already exists; the person you want to meet is already alive; the experience you want to have is available, now; the idea for that brilliant song you want to write is here, now, waiting for you to download the information. The knowledge and insight and joy and connection and love are all wagging their hands in your face, trying to get your attention. The life you want is right here, right now.

What the hell am I talking about? If it's all here, where is it?

Think of it like electricity. Before the invention of the light bulb, most people weren't aware of electricity's existence. It was still here, exactly the same way it is right now, but we hadn't yet woken up to it. It took the invention of the light bulb to bring it to our attention. We had to understand how to manifest it into our reality.

It's not that the things and opportunities that we want in life don't exist yet.

It's that we're not yet aware of their existence (or the fact that we can really have them).

The more practiced you become at being present and connected to Source Energy, the more available you are to download ideas and seize opportunities that you might miss out on if you're all wrapped up in the endless chatter in your head.

There's a great Hindu story about a lady who wanted to meet the god Krishna. So she went into the forest, closed her eyes, and prayed and meditated on making the god appear and lo and behold, Krishna came wandering down the forest path toward her. But when Krishna tapped the lady on the shoulder, she, without opening her eyes, told him to get lost because she was busy meditating on a very important goal.

When we get so wrapped up in our heads, we miss out on what's available to us right now in the moment. Stop and notice how you feel right now. Feel your breath moving in and out of your body. Feel the air on your skin. Feel your heart beating. Your eyes seeing. Your ears hearing. Notice the energy inside and outside of you buzzing. Shut off your thoughts and feel your connection to Source. B-r-e-a-t-h-e. Even if you've got bone-chilling credit card debts or you haven't spoken to your mother in six years, right now, in this moment, you can find peace and joy in that which simply is.

As adults with responsibilities like bodies to care for and mortgages to pay, there's some value in taking a side trip away from the present moment every once in a while; sometimes we need to think about and plan for the future, as well as study the past in order to learn from it or laugh about it or to bury it out back and let it go forever. And if we just stopped by for the occasional visits to the future and past, that would be one thing, but the amount of time we spend chewing on junk-food thoughts about what-ifs and how-comes—Lawd help us!

The more time you spend in the moment, the richer your life will be. Being present gets you out of your head and connects you to Source Energy, which raises your frequency, which attracts things of like frequency to you. And all of those high-frequency things and experiences are already here, just waiting for you to join the party, all you have to do is shut up, show up, and usher them in.

CHAPTER 4:

THE BIG SNOOZE

Wanting to be someone else is a waste of the person you are.
—Kurt Cobain; you know who this one is, right?

When I first started getting into self-helpery, there was lots of talk about something called the "Ego" that confused the hell out of me. I always thought that Ego was about being conceited and braggy and all, "I'm gonna talk on and on and on about how great I am and then I'm gonna show you my muscles." Meanwhile, even though arrogance and conceit (which are different from self-love and confidence, BTW) are part of the Ego, they're not, as I later learned, the whole dealio.

In the self-help/spiritual community, "Ego" is used to refer to the shadow self, or the false self, or the self that's acting like a weenie. It's the part of us that's driving the bus when we do things like sabotage our happiness by cheating on our husbands or wives because deep down we don't feel worthy of being loved, or that refuses to follow our hearts and pursue an acting career because we're terrified to be seen for who we really are or that goes on and on and on and on about how great we are and shows off our muscles because we're insecure and need lots of outside validation that we're good enough.

In other words, there's more than one way to go on an ego trip.

From here on out, I'm going to refer to the Ego as the Big Snooze. Or BS for short. I think it'll be less confusing. Plus I think it's more appropriate, since the leading cause of sucking (staying broke, dating morons, uncontrollably crying in public because we hate our lives) is that we haven't yet woken up to how truly powerful we are or to how massively abundant our Universe is.

Alrighty, so, moving forward.

The Big Snooze operates according to your limiting false beliefs. This is the garbage that was stuffed into your subconscious as a kid that doesn't ring true for you, as well as the decisions you've made about yourself that are less-than flattering or empowering. It gets validation from outside sources (I'm doing this to win your love, your opinion of me is more important than my opinion of me), it's reactive (My circumstances control my life, I am a victim), fear-based, and extremely committed to keeping you safely confined within the reality you've created based on these limiting false beliefs (otherwise known as your comfort zone). The Big Snooze lives in the past and in the future and believes you are separate from everything around you.

Your true self or your higher self or your superhero self (your non-BS self), on the other hand, is the part of you that operates according to your connection to Source Energy. It gets validation from within (I love and trust myself, this feels right to me, I have a purpose, I am loved), it's proactive (I'm in control of my life, I think I'll head on out and kick me some ass), love-based, and is committed to creating a reality based on your limitless potential—as soon as you wake up from the Big Snooze. Your true self lives in the present (not stuck in your head), totally believes in miracles and is one with the Universe.

We all experience life in varying degrees from both perspectives, and while I seriously doubt there's anyone who's totally Snooze-free, most people are so wrapped up in the BS that they're settling for realities that are waaaaaaaay beneath what's available to them.

Very few people are even aware of what's available, however, because we live in a fear-based society that loves to get all uppity toward people who wake up from the Big Snooze, blast out of their comfort zones, and follow their hearts into the great unknown. Oftentimes, taking great leaps of faith is labeled as irresponsible or selfish or insane (until you succeed of course, then you're brilliant). This is because:

• •

Watching someone else totally go for it can be incredibly upsetting to the person who's spent a lifetime building a solid case for why they themselves can't.

• •

I'm obviously generalizing, and there are plenty of people out there cheering us on, but one of the first things you might have to deal with when you decide to wake up from the Big Snooze and make massive positive changes in your life is disapproval from other people who are snoring away. Especially the people closest to you, lame as this may sound.

They may express their discomfort in all sorts of ways: anger, hurt,

bafflement, criticism, snorting every time you talk about your new
business or your new friends, constant remarks about how you're not
the way you used to be, brow furrowing, worrying, teasing, blocking
you from all social media outlets, etc.

*Shirley, are you really going to quit your secure, corporate job to open a nail
salon when you've got two children, a mortgage, and high blood pressure? So few
new businesses succeed, especially in this economy—aren't you worried about
what will happen to your family if you fail?*

Of course Shirley is worried about what will happen to her family if she fails! She wakes up every night seized by panic about it, but
she's moving past her fear to create something she's really psyched
about, rather than dying a slow painful death hanging around the
watercooler with you, whining about how dry the cake was at
the birthday party your boss threw for you in the conference room
last week.

Even though they're often doing it out of love and concern, having
others smear their fear and worry all over you is the last thing you
need when you're strengthening your superhero muscles to step out
and take some risks, so I highly recommend keeping your mouth shut
around people who are gonna bring you down. Instead, seek out those
who are already totally kicking butt (or who are lifting up their foot
to do so), or people who you know will be supportive, and confide in
them. Because you'll have your own internal freak show to deal with
as you try to overcome the objections from your own BS.

The Big Snooze is like an overprotective Italian mother who not
only doesn't want you to ever go outside, but who wants you to live
with her forever. Her intentions are good, but fully fear-based. As long
as you stay inside the familiar, risk-free zone of your present reality, the
Big Snooze is content, but should you try and sneak past her to attend
the rockin' party outside, your overprotective, controlling mother is
going to claw, scratch, scream, bite, hurl her body in front of your

rapidly approaching new life—basically she's going to do whatever she can to stop you. And it ain't gonna be pretty.

It's like when you quit smoking or doing drugs and go into withdrawal. Finally, you've taken a leap and done something that's going to massively improve your life, and for days, sometimes weeks, you feel worse than you did when you were a wild child. You're hacking up all this nasty crap, ridding your body of toxins, shaking, sweating, puking, wondering why on Earth you thought this was a good idea. It's really fun.

Same goes for when we rid ourselves of limiting subconscious beliefs that have been holding us back and take a giant leap outside our comfort zone. It's a detox of such staggering proportions that sometimes it can feel like The Universe is conspiring against us—trees fall on our cars, our computers crash, we find our significant others in bed with our best friends, we get our identities stolen, we get the flu, our roofs cave in, we sit in gum—when in reality, The Big Snooze is creating chaos in an attempt to self-sabotage and keep everything as is, instead of moving forward into unknown, yet desperately wanted, new territory. Every successful person knows this and has been through this.

· ·

When taking great leaps forward, life often turns to shit before it turns to Shinola.

· ·

I realize this might seem a bit far-fetched, but remember, you create your reality. And you've spent a lifetime creating the one you presently have largely based on your limiting beliefs. When you decide to re-wire these beliefs, go for what's truly in your heart and do a massive overhaul on yourself and your world, you're basically murdering the Big Snooze. And she is going to come at you, rolling pin raised high over her head, to beat you back into your old life. We are very

powerful creatures who create our realities through focused energy, and
should our subconscious mind decide to focus that energy at stopping
ourselves from taking a risk because it's freaking out and terrified,
things can get a little crazy around here.

**The Big Snooze will do everything it can to stop you
from changing and growing, especially since you're
attempting to obliterate the very identity that you
and everyone else has come to know as "you."**

Never underestimate the power of the Big Snooze scorned.

Sometimes the Big Snooze sets up emotional blocks to try and stop
us, other times she gets physical. I have a client who decided to quit his
ho-hum yet high-paying job to start his dream company from scratch.
He had no idea where to start, what he wanted to do or how he was
going to pull it off, and regardless of the fact that he had a family that
was counting on him, no guarantees and even fewer leads, he quit his
secure job and went for it because he was determined to create a life he
loved. That's when the BS hit the fan—he got not one, but two flat tires
after leaving a coaching session with me, his babysitter ran into his
wife's car while driving his car, the water main under his kitchen
exploded, and right before his first big deal went through, he got hit by
a freakin bus (I'm pleased to report he's fine). But even with all those
extremely convincing excuses to say *Ok, fine, screw it, you win,* he never
gave up. Today he finds himself being his own boss, doing what he loves,
traveling the world, negotiating multi-million dollar deals, making a
huge difference in his clients' lives, being creative and setting an excellent example for his kids about living life on purpose.

A record producer I worked with decided to build her own recording studio. She put all her money and effort into buying all the
recording equipment, instruments, amps, soundproofing, etc., only to

have the entire thing burn to the ground almost immediately after it was completed. Instead of closing the shades, getting into bed and sucking her thumb for the next two years, she raised the money she needed to rebuild an even better studio and is now rocking so hard that she gets to hand pick the musicians she works with and basically live out her fantasy life.

So if you finally decide to quit your soul-crushing job and start the pastry shop of your dreams, be not upset if a truck drives through your front window into your scones. Instead of taking this as a sign that you shouldn't have opened your shop, take it to mean that you're ridding yourself of your BS and moving in the right direction.

Growth ain't for weenies, but it's no where near as painful as living the life you're living right now if you're not *really* going for it. If you want to take control of your life and turn it into something as spectacularly "you" as have the people I described above, stop at nothing. Have faith. Trust that your new life is already here and is far better than the old. Hang tight if the Big Snooze pitches a fit. Whatever happens, stay the course, because there's nothing cooler than watching your entire reality shift into one that is the perfect expression of you.

CHAPTER 5:

SELF-PERCEPTION IS A ZOO

I'm okay, I'm not okay.
—The title of my friend Cynthia's yet-to-be-written
autobiography

I have a friend who's a professional speaker. She's the kind of person who is so articulate, so powerful and bright and naturally captivating, that she could be standing at the counter, ordering a burrito and I'd get all teary-eyed: "That's right! No refried beans! You heard the woman!" So imagine my surprise when, after one of her talks, she plunked herself down next to me and demanded to know how boring it was. I also have gorgeous friends who think they're hideous looking, brilliant clients who one moment think they're God's gift to mankind and the next need to be talked off the ledge of self-proclaimed ineptitude, and an entrepreneurial neighbor who can't decide if she's a financial powerhouse or if she's about to cause her family to start living underneath a bridge.

Self-perception is a zoo.

We spend our lives drifting between glimpses of our own, infinite glory and the fear that not only are we totally incapable/unworthy/lazy/horrible, but that it's only a matter of time before someone blows the whistle on us. We torture ourselves incessantly, and for what purpose? If we can glimpse the glory (and I know you can), why do we waste our precious time giving any energy to the other options? Wouldn't life be so much more fun, productive, and sexy if we fully embraced our magnificently delightful selves?

· ·

It's just as easy to believe we're awesome as it is to believe we're giant sucking things.

· ·

Takes the same amount of energy. The same amount of focus. So why do we choose all the drama?

Have you ever noticed how when someone you admire goes out and does something phenomenal, you're happy for her or him, but you're not surprised—*of course they did something phenomenal, they're a phenomenal person!* But to get yourself to see how amazing you are is like pushing a giant marshmallow up a hill. *Yes, there we go, we are up, we are awesome! Ooop! We're sagging—we are sagging on the left! Push it up. There we go. We are all good! Wait, now we're sagging on the right . . .* We run around, taking one step forward and fourteen steps back when it's so unnecessary.

Instead, try seeing yourself through the eyes of someone who admires *you*. They get it. They believe in you leaps and bounds. They aren't connected to your insecurities and negative beliefs about yourself. All they see is your true glory and potential. Become one of your own die-hard fans, look at yourself from the outside, where all your self doubts can't crawl all over you, and behold what shines through.

You get to choose how you perceive your reality. So why, when it comes to perceiving yourself, would you choose to see anything other than a super huge rock star of a creature?

You are a badass. You were one when you came screaming onto this planet and you are one now. The Universe wouldn't have bothered with you otherwise. You can't screw up so majorly that your badassery disappears. *It is who you are.* It's who you always will be. It's not up for negotiation.

You are loved. Massively. Ferociously. Unconditionally. The Universe is totally freaking out about how awesome you are. It's got you wrapped in a warm gorilla hug of adoration. It wants to give you everything you desire. It wants you to be happy. It wants you to see what it sees in you.

You are perfect. To think anything less is as pointless as a river thinking that it's got too many curves or that it moves too slowly or that its rapids are too rapid. Says who? You're on a journey with no defined beginning, middle or end. There are no wrong twists and turns. There is just being. And your job is to be as you as you can be. This is why you're here. To shy away from who you truly are would leave the world you-less. You are the only you there is and ever will be. I repeat, *you are the only you there is and ever will be.* Do not deny the world its one and only chance to bask in your brilliance.

We are all perfect in our own, magnificent, fucked-up ways. Laugh at yourself. Love yourself and others. Rejoice in the cosmic ridiculousness.

PART 2:
HOW TO
EMBRACE
YOUR INNER
BADASS

CHAPTER 6:

LOVE THE ONE YOU IS

If we really love ourselves, everything in our life works.
—Louise Hay; author, publisher, the Godmother of Self-Help
who was doing it way back when it still wasn't cool

I was hanging out at my brother Bobby's house one day, lying on the couch, watching his then-two-year-old son waddle around. At one point, someone knocked something off the coffee table, and my little nephew bent down to pick it up. Bobby turned to me and said, "Did you see that? The guy knows exactly how it's done. He bends at the knees, keeps his back straight, hips squared, stomach tight—flawless!"

Thrilled to have such a willing and skilled Exhibit A, Bobby then proceeded to spend the next couple of minutes dropping more things on the floor—a spoon, a TV remote, an empty can of beer—and my nephew, in perfect form, continued to pick it all up as my brother kept up a running commentary on his posture, muscle usage, seriousness of manner, and the fact that my nephew was pulling it all off with great dignity even though his diaper was sagging.

"It's incredible. The kid could flip over a car without straining his back. I can barely pull up my pants without having to be rushed to the hospital."

When we're born, we have an instinctual understanding of some of the most important basics of life that includes, and goes way beyond, bending at our knees, instead of our lower backs, to pick a beer can up off the floor. We're born knowing how to trust our instincts, how to breathe deeply, how to eat only when we're hungry, how to not care about what anyone thinks of our singing voices, dance moves, or hair-dos, we know how to play, create, and love without holding back. Then, as we grow and learn from the people around us, we replace many of these primal understandings with negative false beliefs, fear, shame, and self-doubt. Then we wind up in emotional and physical pain. Then we either numb our pain with drugs, sex, booze, TV, Cheetos, etc. Or we settle for mediocrity. OR we rise to the occasion, remember how truly mighty we are, and set out to relearn everything we knew at the beginning all over again.

It's like we're born with a big bag of money, more than enough to fund any dream of ours, and instead of following our instincts and our hearts, we invest in what other people believe we should invest in. Some people invest in believing they're too old to go out clubbing when they love nothing more than the boogie, some invest in being tough and too-cool-for-school when all they want is love and connec-tion, some invest in being ashamed of their sexuality instead of being their gloriously gay selves. As we continue to buy into these things that aren't even true for us, our inner fortunes dwindle away, and it isn't until we reconnect with who we *truly* are and start investing in what's true for us that we start to live rich, full, authentic lives.

And while there are countless ways that we rip ourselves off, there's one way in particular that is, without a doubt, the most rampant and the most devastating of all: **we invest everything we've got in believing that we're not good enough.**

We arrive here as perfect little bundles of joy and then set about the task of learning to un-love ourselves! How unbelievably ridiculous is that?! Self-love, the simplest yet most powerful thing *ever*, flies right out the window when we start taking in outside information.

I'm not talking about conceit or narcissism, because those things also come from fear and a lack of self-love. I'm talking about a deep connection with our highest selves, and an unshakable ability to forgive our lowest. I'm talking about loving ourselves enough to let go of guilt, resentment, and criticism and embrace compassion, joy, and gratitude.

....

When we're happy and all in love with ourselves, we can't be bothered with the bullshit (our own or other people's).

....

Imagine what our world would be like if everyone loved themselves so much that they weren't threatened by other people's opinions or skin colors or sexual preferences or talents or education or possessions or lack of possessions or religious beliefs or customs or their general tendency to just be whoever the hell they are. Imagine how different your reality would be (and the reality of everyone surrounding you) if you woke up every morning certain of your own lovability and your critically important role on this planet. And if you poo-pooed shame, guilt, self-doubt, and self-loathing *and allowed yourself to be, do, and have everything your little heart desired.*

THAT'S the kind of world I want to live in.

In the interest of perpetuating such radical, reality-altering self-love, here are some of the best ways to win yourself over again:

1. APPRECIATE HOW SPECIAL YOU ARE

There will never be anyone exactly like you. You were given special gifts and talents to share with the world, and even though everybody has special gifts and talents, nobody will use theirs quite the same way you do. You have a way of being in the world and a perspective that's unique to you. You are the only one who thinks your thoughts the way you think them. You have created your own unique reality and are living your life according to your own unique path. You are the only you that will ever be. You are kind of a big deal.

2. DROWN YOURSELF IN AFFIRMATIONS

Trust me, I wouldn't do this to you unless I had to, but affirmations work. You don't have to say them in the mirror, you don't have to hug yourself or buy a special rainbow journal with a lock on it to write them down in, but if you want to turn the ship around, you need to rewire your brain and train it to think differently. And this is what affirmations can do for you.

Figure out which affirmations you need to hear the most and repeat them all day long in your head, in the car, while you're walking down the street pretending to be on the phone, under your breathe in line at the DMV. Write them on Post-it notes and stick them around your house, on your mirrors, in your refrigerator, in your car. Write down your favorite affirmations ten times every morning and ten times every night before you go to bed and say them out loud.

Here are some affirmations specific to self-love. Pick one or two that work for you and pummel yourself with them:

- I deserve and receive massive amounts of love every moment of every day.

- I am one with The Universe. The Universe is awesome and so am I.

- My heart is open. Love pours in and out.

- I receive all the good that life has to offer me.

- I am brilliant, bright, and beautiful.

- I love how tall I am and I love the size of my ass.

Or whatever. If none of these work, come up with some that don't make you gag but that strike a nerve with you. *The more emotion you feel around what you're saying, the more power it will have to bring about positive change.* And yes, at the beginning it may feel like you're lying to yourself, but the truth is, you're living the lie, so the affirmations get you back to truth.

This can't be just rattling off nonsense—you have to feel it and want it and get worked up by it in order for it to work.

3. DO THINGS YOU LOVE

When you constantly deny yourself the people, food, things, and experiences that make you feel the most alive, that sends a pretty lousy message home.

Look at your life and see where you're letting yourself down. If you hear yourself saying things like "I love going out to see live music! I can't remember the last time I did it," *make time.*

We're all busy, but it's the people who make enjoying their lives a priority who, um, enjoy their lives. Right now, there are thousands of people all over the world at yoga retreats overlooking the ocean, dancing their asses off at outdoor music festivals or whooping it up on the Disney Cruise of their dreams. Really listen to how you speak and pay attention to what you do, and make a conscious effort to increase your joy in whatever capacity you can. It can be anything from spending a weekday afternoon with a great friend to quitting your hateful job to buying a pair of completely impractical but completely awesome new shoes to going on a surf vacation in Costa Rica. It's about being proactive about creating a life you love instead of meekly living the one you think you're stuck with. Give yourself the gift of a joyous life while you're still among the living.

Also, if you're the kind of person who puts everyone else's needs first, start putting yours up front. Those who are used to you being their personal assistant will still love you, even though they'll be somewhat grouchy about you not waiting on them hand and foot anymore. Buy a new pair of jeans, open a savings account, hire someone to do your dishes, make your kids clean out the cat box—you aren't a selfish person for taking care of yourself, just a happier one. Take care of yourself as if you're the most awesome person you've ever met.

4. FIND A REPLACEMENT

We've gotten so used to our negative knee-jerk reactions to ourselves that we never think to question them—we simply take them as the truth the whole truth and nothing but the truth. But once we become aware of our thought patterns and behaviors, we can consciously change them. So start paying attention:

What runs through your mind when you look in the mirror?

What happens inside you when you see someone totally succeeding at something you'd love to do but have never let yourself try?

What do you think and feel when you walk up to a group of really good-looking, successful people?

Or when you try your best to pull something off and you fail?

Or when you get dumped by someone who is totally awesome? And hot?

Or when you walk around all day with your fly open?

Or when you leave your coffee on the roof of your car and drive off?

Or when you let a friend down?

Or when you stub your toe on the kitchen table for the tenth time?

Or when you forget your dad's birthday?

Or when you snap at someone who didn't quite deserve it as harshly as you gave it to them?

Notice the verbiage that runs through your mind when you're being the most heinous to yourself and come up with a new-and-improved response.

For example, if every time you look in the mirror, your first thought is *yikes,* make a conscious effort to change it to *hi, gorgeous!*

If you have a complicated relationship with your father and beat yourself up every time you say something awful to him, replace *I'm a monster* with *I'm just a little bunny, working through my issues.* And then, of course, apologize to him.

If your standard response to screwing something up is *ugh, Her Royal Clumsiness strikes again*, replace it with *what can I learn from this?*

The most important thing is to free yourself from the drama and the conviction that your current version of yourself is the truth. I don't care if you're all, "that's easy for you to say; you don't have a nose that makes it look like someone parked a yacht on your face." Because one day you could see some fancy and famous fashion model with a nose far bigger than yours is who decided she was gorgeous anyway, and suddenly you'll feel beautiful and confident and all proud of your nose when, just the day before, you were considering getting it sawed off.

This is how ridiculous we are.

Do not spend your life clinging to the insulting decisions you've made about yourself. Instead, make the conscious choice to replace them with new and improved ones.

5. DITCH THE SELF-DEPRECATING HUMOR

Incessant self-deprecating humor is for losers. I get it—it can be hilariously funny and I'm totally guilty of it from time to time and there's nobody I'd more enjoy backing over with my car than the guy who can't laugh at himself, but I'm talking about the nonstop, self-flagellating, I Suckfest. Ripping on yourself gets old. Fast. Especially if it's your shtick. So if you're one of those people who falls back on making fun of yourself, every hour on the hour, not only are you basically begging people to think you're a loser, but you're begging yourself to think you're a loser. It's like hitting yourself over and over with a crowbar. Why on earth would you do that to your awesome self?

What you tell yourself on a daily basis is more powerful than you know. Seemingly harmless jokes, over time, turn into seriously destructive beliefs. Our thoughts become our words, our words become our beliefs, our beliefs become our actions, our actions become our habits, and our habits become our realities. So if your favorite joke is that you couldn't get a date if you demanded one at gunpoint, and you spend every Saturday night alone, perhaps you should come up with a new one-liner.

And most importantly, constantly making fun of yourself is such a cheap way to be funny. Anyone can do it. So push yourself to come up with a new script. Your confidence, and we humor snobs, will thank you.

6. LET THE LOVE IN

Receive compliments gracefully instead of countering with a disclaimer such as, "Oh, this ratty old thing?" Try this instead: "Thank you." Period.

Take care of your body, too. We, if you're anything like me, run around doing all our busy work with our poor bodies flapping behind us like old wind socks. When we're pressed for time, it's often the first thing to get overlooked. "I've got five meetings today, I'll do my yoga tomorrow and have a power bar for lunch." Meanwhile, during our little sojourn here on earth, we need our bodies more than they need us. Say nice things about your body, dress it up, and take it out. Give it hot sex, luxurious baths, and massages. Move it, stretch it, nourish it, hydrate it, pay attention to it—The better our bodies feel, the happier and more productive we are.

7. DON'T COMPARE YOURSELF TO OTHERS

Have you ever done something that you're so proud of and feel all on top of the world about it until you see that someone else has done something similar that, in your mind, is better, and all of a sudden you feel sad?

••

Comparison is the fastest way to take all the fun out of life.

••

It's none of your business what other people are doing. All that matters is that you're enjoying yourself and pleased with what you're creating. It's precisely your uniqueness that makes you awesome— deciding that someone else's uniqueness is better than your own isn't exactly being your own best buddy about things.

Can you imagine what our world would be like if our biggest heroes succumbed to the perils of comparison? If Marilyn Monroe compared herself to Kate Moss and decided she needed to lose her curves? Or if the guys in Led Zeppelin compared themselves to Mozart? *Dude. That guy's huge. Way huger than we'll ever be and he doesn't even have a drummer. I think we should get rid of ours and maybe add some harps while we're at it.*

You are more than enough. Avoid comparison like the plague.

8. FORGIVE YOURSELF (LISTEN UP! THIS ONE'S EXTREMELY IMPORTANT.)

You have screwed up in the past. You will screw up again. Every human is born with the ability to make spectacular mistakes. You are not alone, screwing up is not your special skill. Get over it. Dragging around guilt and self-criticism is beyond unhealthy and is utterly pointless, not to mention boring. You aren't a better person for feeling guilty or bad about yourself, just a sadder one.

Get clear on this one truth: guilt, shame, and self-criticism are some of the most destructive forces in your life, which is why forgiving yourself is one of the most powerful. Here's an excellent way to do it:

Think of a specific thing that you did that you feel badly about. Call it up in your mind and feel it in your body. Repeat the following over and over while thinking of it and really feel what you're saying to yourself:

Holding on to my bad feelings about this is doing nothing but harming me, and everyone else, and preventing me from enjoying my life fully. I am an awesome person. I choose to enjoy my life. I choose to let this go.

Repeat this until you feel a sense of freedom and lightness around your issue. It may take a day or a week or several months or it could happen right away. But however long it takes, do it, because if you want to be free, you have to put in the time. (See Chapter 15 for more tips on forgiveness and letting go.) And if you need to apologize to someone, pick up the phone.

9. LOVE YOURSELF

Because it's the Holy Grail of happiness.

CHAPTER 7:

I KNOW YOU ARE BUT WHAT AM I?

I'm not offended by all the dumb blonde jokes because I know I'm not dumb.
I also know I'm not blonde.

—Dolly Parton; singer, songwriter, actress, altruist,
businesswoman, bright shiny light

A friend of mine—a brilliant writer—once called me in a panic when she suddenly became frozen with fear over the subject matter of the book she was working on and could no longer bring herself to write it.

Her book was, among many other splendid things, very personal, dark, and twisted, and my friend was concerned that it was too much. That it was crossing the line.

That she was exposing herself as a giant weirdo pervert freak.

This brings up something that's SO important to have a firm grasp on if you're going to get anywhere near reaching your full potential in this life as a writer, an artist, a businessperson, a parent, a butcher, a baker, a candlestick-maker or as a fully realized and evolved human being in general:

DO NOT WASTE YOUR PRECIOUS TIME GIVING ONE SINGLE CRAP ABOUT WHAT ANYBODY ELSE THINKS OF YOU.

Imagine how liberating that would be!

Other people's opinions motivate every move we make in our teens and our twenties. And, as we age, if we're moving in the right direction, our obsession with how we're perceived by others begins to trickle away, but very few of us are able to escape its pointless grasp completely.

Meanwhile, the truth is, the only questions you ever need to consider when making decisions about your life are:

1. Is this something I want to be, do, or have?

2. Is this going to take me in the direction I want to go (not *should* go)?

3. Is this going to screw over* anybody else in the process?

*The definition of *screwing someone over* is taking their money and doing a lousy job or destroying their water source or enslaving populations, things like that—your mother being disappointed or your father disapproving or your friends being outraged does not qualify as screwing someone over.

We throw a wet blanket of ho-hummery over our lives when we live in fear of what others might think, instead of in celebration of who we are.

Yes, it's part of our survival instinct to care—get booted from the tribe and you'll freeze to death or starve or be eaten by wolves. But because we have big brains and the ability to manifest anything we set our minds to, there is another version that's equally plausible: Get booted from the tribe and start, or find, another tribe that's more your style. You could not only wind up doing what you love surrounded by people you adore who you actually relate to, but you might one day realize you can no longer remember the names of the people whose approval you so desperately thought you would die without.

Nobody who ever accomplished anything big or new or worth raising a celebratory fist in the air did it from their comfort zone. They risked ridicule and failure and sometimes even death. Think of the Wright brothers. Can you imagine how that whole thing went down?

Margaret: Did you hear about poor Susan?
Ruth: Susan Wright?
Helen: Such a disgrace. Poor thing.
Ruth: What happened?
Margaret: Well, her sons . . .
Helen: As if she hasn't suffered enough. Birthing two boys as big as buffaloes, and now this . . .
Margaret: Seems her two sons . . .
Helen: You gonna eat the rest of your tapioca pudding? Mind if I help myself?

Ruth: Tell me already, Margaret!

Margaret: Well, this is going to sound as crazy as it is but they . . .

Helen: And now her sons think they can fly. Such a shame.

Margaret: . . . Her sons think—they think they can fly.

Ruth: Think they can fly?

Margaret: Yes, they think they can fly. They talk of nothing else.

Helen: She just had the house painted, too. They'll probably have to move out of town now. . . .

Once you step away from the herd and let your true self shine, you'll probably find yourself in front of the opinion firing squad (especially if what you want to do is extraordinary and outside of everyone's comfort zones), which is why so many people run screaming from the lives they'd so love to live. Merely allowing yourself to be seen is a risk. I mean, look at how we treat celebrities—their every move is picked apart and passed around and discussed and judged and photographed without makeup on. It's a wonder that only half of them spend time in rehab.

••

You are responsible for what you say and do. You are not responsible for whether or not people freak out about it.

••

Two people can walk out of the same movie, one person clinging to the walls, bloodshot and devastated, leaving a trail of tissues, more moved by this film than any other film in the history of cinema while the other person goes marching up to the ticket counter and demands her money back because she thought it was the worst piece of garbage to ever be projected onto a screen.

One movie, two very different experiences. Why?

Because it's not about the movie, it's about the moviegoers.

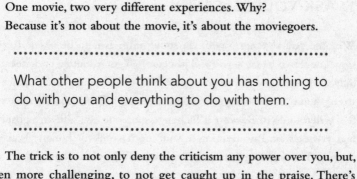

What other people think about you has nothing to do with you and everything to do with them.

The trick is to not only deny the criticism any power over you, but, even more challenging, to not get caught up in the praise. There's nothing wrong with blushingly accepting a compliment, but if you find yourself always seeking outside approval that you're good enough or cool enough or talented enough or worthy enough, you're screwed. Because if you base your self-worth on what everyone else thinks of you, you hand all your power over to other people and become dependent on a source outside of yourself for validation. Then you wind up chasing after something you have no control over, and should that something suddenly place its focus somewhere else, or change its mind and decide you're no longer very interesting, you end up with a full-blown identity crisis.

All that matters is what's true for you, and if you can stay connected to that without straying, you will be a mighty superhero.

Everything else is just other people's perception of reality, and that is none of your business.

So how can you truly not care what other people think and be your most powerful Self?

1. ASK YOURSELF WHY

Why are you about to say or do something? Is it to be liked? To put someone down because you feel insecure? To get someone back because they made a fat joke about your mother? Or is it coming from a place of strength and truth? Are you doing it because it'll be fun? Because you feel called to do it? Because it'll change someone else's life in a positive, martyr-free way? Pay attention to your motivations (be honest). Practice coming from a place of integrity and you will be victorious.

2. ALWAYS DO YOUR BEST

There's no faster way to fall prey to outside input than when you're feeling insecure. And there's no better way to feel insecure than knowing you half-assed something or don't really believe in what you're doing. No matter what it is—raising your prices or raising your children—if you do the absolute best you possibly can, and come from a place of integrity, then you can be proud of yourself and not give a damn what anyone else thinks.

3. TRUST YOUR INTUITION

Birds use their intuition to navigate their way to breeding grounds halfway around the world. Deer and rabbits and other prey type beasts use their intuition to avoid running into predators. The average human, on the other hand, will take the advice of their drunk-before-noon neighbor across the street instead of doing what deep down we know is best. How many times have you thought in hindsight, *I knew I should have listened to my gut!?*

You have an incredible, inner guidance tool that you can use whenever you need it. Tell everyone to shut up and go away, get quiet, give yourself room to feel and think. You have all the answers inside of you. Practice sharpening your intuition, take the time to strengthen your connection to Source Energy, and trust that you know what's best for you. The more centered and tuned-in you are, the mightier you will be (look for more tips on how to do this later in this book).

4. FIND A TEMPORARY ROLE MODEL

Find a mentor or a hero or a role model. Get clear on why this person is impressive and inspiring to you, and when faced with a challenge that leaves you guessing how to react, ask yourself, *What would my hero do?*

Not caring what others think is a muscle that can take some time to build up, so use this trick while you're still getting strong, and before you know it, you'll be able to ditch your hero and start asking yourself, *What would I do?*

5. LOVE YOURSELF

No matter what anyone else thinks.

IMPORTANT NOTE ABOUT OUTSIDE OPINIONS: While you are unauthorized to base your self-worth on what other people think, it doesn't mean you should miss out on the opportunity to benefit from outside input altogether. Especially input from those who know you well.

There is such a thing as constructive criticism, and constructive complimenting. But whether or not they are constructive depends on you.

For example, if people have been telling you for years that you're a hothead, that they feel like they can't be open with you because the second you disagree with them you blow up in their faces, ask yourself *Is this true (be honest)? Can I use this information to better myself and the lives of others?* If the answer is yes, commit to making the necessary changes; if the answer is no, let it go.

Same goes for compliments. If people constantly tell you you're a good listener, ask yourself, *Is this compliment true for me? Can I use this information to better myself and the lives of others?* Again, if the answer is yes, figure out how you can capitalize on it; if the answer is no, let it go.

Sometimes it's easier for other people to see what we can't see ourselves, so if they can help us connect with our truths and live happier, more authentic lives, then it's worth taking the time to listen.

It still ultimately comes down to what's true for you, however, so the more connected to your inner truth you are, the easier it will be to use outside opinions to your advantage, rather than let them rule your life.

CHAPTER 8:

WHAT ARE YOU DOING HERE?

*The big question is whether you are going to be able
to say a hearty yes to your adventure.*

**—Joseph Campbell; American mythologist, author whose
books/ideas influenced the making of *Star Wars***

Getting clear about what your unique purpose is can be the difference
between living a happy, fulfilled life of abundance, choice, and expan-
siveness or living in the restrictive veal pen of your own indecision and
tired old excuses.

A gift, of course, is meant to be given, which is why it's so brutal when we can't figure out what ours is, or when we know what it is, but we're too lame to act on it: here we have the perfect gift to share with the world, just bursting to be opened, and we keep it sitting there, wrapped tightly in a box, growing old and gathering dust. Oh the waste! The agony!

Meanwhile, the joy of giving someone the perfect gift is unparalleled. We all know how it feels, hopping back and forth from foot to foot, wringing our hands, practically peeing in our pants, begging them to open it. OPEN IT ALREADY! *Jesus H. Christ . . . here let me freakin' do it!* The power of giving is so strong that the excitement and the good feelings are often greater for the giver than for the receiver.

Which is why, when you find your calling and you design your life in such a way that you can share your gifts with the world on a consistent basis, you feel like a rock star.

....

When we share what we were brought here to give, we are in alignment with our highest, most powerful selves.

....

Most people, however, wander through their lives giving the tasteful candle version of their gifts. You know—they don't show up to the party empty-handed or anything; they present their somewhat flaccid gift to the world, receive a warm hug, and an, "Oh, you shouldn't have," in return, but they don't knock it out of the park. For example, they get a job doing something that they either hate or that's a bit of a yawn but is, you know, okay. It affords them a life that covers the basics as long as they don't go too crazy. They do fun stuff but not as much as they'd like because they don't have the money. Or the time. Or the belief that they deserve to. They have little victories here and there, they meet their sales quota and win the six-day cruise to the Bahamas or rack up enough miles to go stay with their aunt and see the Olympics or finally sit down and write an entire song that they may or may not ever record or perform, but they never truly go for it and create a life that really lights them up. They basically Big Snooze their lives away.

Every single person is born with unique and valuable gifts to share with the world. Once we figure out what ours are, and decide to live our lives putting them to use, that's when, and only when, the real party begins. Living a life on purpose is available to *everyone*. So if you're struggling or settling or completely confused about what you're supposed to do with your life, know that the answer is already here. It exists and so does the life you can't wait to create. You just need to get some clarity first.

There are entire books written on finding your calling (some of the best of which I share in the Resources section in the back of this book and on my website), but the following are a few of my favorite tips.

Keep in mind there's no right way to go about this. Everyone's journey is unique, but we're all trying to get to the same place—the place where we feel happiest, the most alive, and the most like ourselves.

Even if you've nailed the perfect career for yourself, read on, because these tips can help you in all areas of your life.

How to get clear on who you are and what your calling is:

1. BE THE ALIEN

Imagine that you're an alien floating around in outer space and you suddenly swoop down to Earth and inhabit your own body. As the alien, everything about this life is new to you. You look around—what do you see? What is this person who you've inhabited so obviously awesome at? What do they have the most fun doing? What connections do they have? What resources and opportunities are available to them?

As the alien, to whom everything is new and exciting and there's nothing at risk and no past to lug around, what are you going to do with this incredible new life you've stepped into? How are you going to use this new body and this existence to create something fabulous and awesome starting right now?

This exercise is hugely helpful for getting a new perspective and stepping outside our boring-ass ruts of tired old excuses and lame habits. It can also be very useful in making you aware of all the staggering possibilities and resources that you have at your fingertips and take for granted or do not see. Sometimes it's as simple as looking at things with new eyes to see how astoundingly fortunate we are. Be the alien for twenty-four hours and see what you come up with.

2. TAKE THE FIRST RIGHT STEP

Instead of wasting hours and days and years trying to figure out your perfect next move, just DO something already. Oh the time we waste rolling ideas around in our heads, imagining what-ifs, coming up with perfect reasons why and then perfect reasons why not, tearing at our cuticles, making our friends and family carefully screen their calls in case it's us again, wanting to go over some ideas. Get out of your head and take action. You don't have to know exactly where it's going to take you, you just need to start with one thing that feels right and keep following right-feeling things and see where they lead.

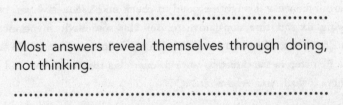

Most answers reveal themselves through doing, not thinking.

When I discovered my calling as a coach I was, ironically, in the midst of a lifelong obsession with figuring out what the hell my purpose was. While I always knew writing was part of it, I also knew I wasn't meant to spend my life locked away in a silent room alone and half-crazed, wrestling words into submission. I wanted something that A) Involved interacting with other people B) Helped people in some sort of direct way C) Was really fun and D) Forced me to bathe, dress and leave my house. That's about all I had to go on, that and my intense desire to figure it out, so when a friend told me I should check out a women's entrepreneurial think-tank group that had just started up, I figured I'd go.

We were all supposed to bring a project to work on, but I had nothing, just the hope that I'd get some ideas from something someone else brought to the table. After sitting there for four weeks watching this roomful of women figure out what they love to do and turn their brilliant ideas into businesses, or grow the businesses they already had, I still had no project of my own. But I did know what I wanted to do. I went up and asked the facilitator if she needed any help, which she did. She hired me, and I started leading these groups, which, after a few years, led to me starting my own coaching practice, which led to me working with clients all over the world which led to me sitting at the kitchen counter writing this book.

No matter how clueless you may feel right now, pay attention to suggestions and opportunities that suddenly present themselves. And notice how you feel—is there something for you that, for whatever reason, feels like it might be good to check out? What have you been saying forever that you'd love to do? Has somebody mentioned a course or a teacher or a book that keeps sticking in your mind? Take the first step in the direction toward something that feels right and see where it leads you. And do it NOW.

3. DO YOUR BEST WHEREVER YOU'RE AT

Once you take this first step, it's possible that you won't land in your dream situation right away. You might land on a stepping-stone. It could be an awesome stepping-stone, or it could be kind of an unpleasant stepping-stone. But no matter where your first step lands you, if you want to keep moving forward, appreciate wherever you're at instead of feeling ashamed or grouchy or impatient about it.

Everything you do along your journey contributes to where you're going.

Let's say you've decided that you're going to go after your fantasy of being a rock star, and you take a job waiting tables so you have the flexibility to travel and play gigs and go in the studio. Clearly, your calling is playing music, not being concerned that some whiney customer's French onion soup is allegedly too cold, but it's essential that you care anyway. Having a good attitude and being grateful for all the things that are helping you live the life of your dreams will not only make your life a more pleasant place to be, and get you bigger tips, but it will also raise your frequency and attract the people and opportunities to you that will take you in the direction you want to go.

This is where really being present in the moment comes in handy. Granted, you may not be onstage in front of thousands doing a split in the air, but remember that you are going for it, you are bravely moving toward your dream, you are surrounded by unthinkable miracles and opportunities. Lean back, relax, and be grateful that you're living on purpose, that you're hanging out in a high frequency, and that everything you need is zooming toward you.

4. DON'T REINVENT THE WHEEL

Look around and see what other people out there are doing. Whose life makes you totally jealous? What things are people doing that you would love to do too? Who do you think is the coolest person ever? You don't need to invent your ideal life from scratch, you just need to figure out what makes you feel alive. So if what someone else is doing sparks your interest, take notice. It could mean that your calling has something in common with theirs.

Get specific about the things in their lives that turn you on. Is it because they get to travel the world? Is it that they have a solid routine? Is it that they have no routine? Is it that they work alone? That they work in the nude? That they get to be outside all day? That they work with their hands? Their eyes? Their ears? Their animals? Their spouse? The more specific you get, the easier it will be to create a picture of what you want.

Read magazines that interest you, talk to as many people as you can, hang out in places where people who share your interests hang out. Put yourself out there and you never know what you might learn that will inform your next move, or whom you might meet that will present you with your next opportunity.

5. DON'T GET CAUGHT UP IN THE THUNDERBOLT HYPE

I think one of the most paralyzing misconceptions is that we're all supposed to have one true calling that comes to us in a mighty flash of
soul-defining insight. While there are those people who've always
known exactly what they want to do, there are a hell of a lot more of
us out there who spend most of our lives, if not all of our lives, wandering around looking under rocks and behind trees for who we are.

Let yourself off the hook if you don't have that one, big, perfect
thing that you know you came here to do (same goes for finding the
one, big, perfect soul mate, BTW), and feel good about the fact that
you'll probably fulfill several callings throughout your life (and possibly relationships).

If you think about it, it makes more sense to evolve as you age anyway. When I think about who I was in my twenties compared to who
I am now, I can't imagine anything more unappealing than going after
some of the things that resonated with me back then.

Follow what feels good in the moment, every moment, and it will
lead you through a most excellent life.

6. LISTEN TO YOUR INTUITION

If you really want to get in touch with who you are and what you love
to do, and who you love to do it with, dedicate some time to tuning
in to your intuition. One of the best ways to do this is to spend five
minutes of quiet, by yourself, every day. We spend the vast majority of
our time moving at full speed ahead, both physically and mentally, and
we literally bulldoze over the very answers we're seeking because they
can't be heard above the din. When you sit quietly and ask, you get an

answer. Eventually. Stick with it, be patient and wait to hear from your inner guidance. You have all the answers you need, you just need to give them the chance to get through to you.

7. FOLLOW YOUR FANTASIES

Now that I've given you all the kinder, gentler ways to figure yourself out, I'm going to suggest something you're probably not going to like so much: Jump in the deep end and follow your fantasies. What do you fantasize about when you're staring out the window of a train, or before you go to sleep at night, or when you're pretending to listen to someone really boring talk your ear off? Are you onstage doing stand-up comedy in front of thousands of hysterical fans? Are you surrounded by your beautiful children in the coziest, happiest home ever? Are you being celebrated for building orphanages around the world? Do this exercise as if money were not an issue. Tap into what brings you great joy instead of what you think you need to do to survive. If you had an unlimited supply of cash, what would you spend your life doing?

Our fantasies are the most revealing peepholes into who we are and what we think is awesome. No matter how out-there and ridiculous they may seem, they mean something to us, and usually represent our biggest and best versions of ourselves.

••

Our fantasies are our realities in an excuse-free world.

••

Meanwhile we'd all be mortified if anyone could read our minds and catch us in the act—"I know, it's totally stupid, I want to sing on Broadway." Well, *is* it really stupid? Someone's out there doing it, so why couldn't you?

Much of the time we pretend we aren't clear on what our calling is when what's really going on is that we're horrified to face it because it seems too big or too impossible to make a living at or completely out of the question for us.

But what if you had the audacity to leave your excuses and your shame about wanting to be huge and fabulous behind and really went for it full-on anyway? What if you decided to do the most outrageous, most exciting thing you ever dared fantasize about, regardless of what anyone, including your terrified self, thought?

THAT would be living.

8. LOVE YOURSELF

Like you're the only you there is.

CHAPTER 9:

LOINCLOTH MAN

*It is better to be hated for what you are
than to be loved for what you are not.*
                    —**André Gide; French author, Nobel Prize winner,**
                                        fearless self-explorer

Every May I go backpacking through the desert wilderness areas of southeast Utah with two longtime friends of mine. It's one of the most magnificent and bizarre places I've ever been: giant, jagged, obscenely pink ridges of rock jut out of the ground like huge slabs of raw meat; white, yellow, and purple towers of sandstone stretch and twist into sculptures made of taffy; deep cracks in the earth's surface form cathedral-like slot canyons whose walls, smoothed over from flash floods and sandstorms, change colors from moment to moment as the sun's rays shift through the narrow opening high above.

It's like the moon. Only cooler.

We merrily trip through this alternate universe, picking up colorful rocks, climbing around on boulders and arguing over which eagle or snake or mountain goat should be awarded Creature of the Day. Because my friends are such excellent navigators, we go deep into the wilderness areas, where there are no trails and even fewer people. In the sixteen years we've been hiking out there, we could practically count the people we've bumped into while backpacking on one hand. Which was why I was so surprised, and dubious, when my friend Tom, who'd gone ahead to find us a place to set up camp for the night, reported that he'd seen someone. "I just met this really wild guy," he said when I caught up with him. "He was wearing nothing but a loincloth and a headband. He was holding a spear, too. Said he'd been living in the canyon for thirteen years."

"Was he riding a magic dragon?"

"I'm serious."

"So where is he?"

"He went off to check his squirrel trap. But he could come back."

"Mmmm hmmmm."

Tom is a lousy liar, and wherever he was taking this joke, he wasn't getting to the punch line fast enough, so I put down my pack and started assembling my tent, only half listening to him. A few minutes into it, as I was bending over to hammer in one of my stakes, I looked through my legs and saw a pair of tanned feet in homemade sandals, strong, naked legs, and a dead squirrel dangling by its tail from a fist. I stood up, spun around, and there he was, Loincloth Man.

What Tom did not mention was that Loincloth Man was totally hot—he was somewhere in his late thirties, had a ripped, lean, savagely tan bod and shaggy brown hair with a matching beard. He fit the part perfectly—Modern Day Tarzan, Slayer of Buffalo and Ladies Alike. Which, stunning as he was, instantly made him a little bit suspect in my mind. That and the fact that his loincloth was impeccably tailored and appeared to be made out of soft Italian leather, not some ratty canyon rabbit. *Would you mind handing that to me so I can have a closer look at it, please?* His whole deal was just a little too cliché. Couldn't he have just worn shorts? And was he *really* gonna eat that squirrel? Still, we gathered around him like a baby pig at the state fair, awestruck by our luck. This time there was no argument; we had clearly found our Creature of the Day.

He was real friendly and answered all of our questions at a slow, deliberate pace, explaining that this and several of the neighboring canyon systems were where he made his home. He told us very matter-of-factly that he found modern society unnecessarily complicated and misguided, so much so that he preferred to live on only what nature provided him, storing his grain in the winter and sleeping in a cave. The thing that struck me more than the fact that he cut his hair with a sharp rock and probably wasn't wearing any undies, was that he was totally unapologetic. There we all were, shifting around, feeling suddenly ridiculous in our expensive hiking boots and UV-protective clothing, while he described how it took him weeks to whittle the bow and arrow he used to kill the deer whose hides now serve as his bedspread.

"Good for him," I thought as I watched him walk away, swinging his squirrel like a purse. He wasn't worrying about what he should be doing or what he was missing out on or what some chick from L.A. thought of his fancy crotch pelt. He was just happy being true to himself, in the moment, in the middle of nowhere.

I wanna be like loincloth man.

LOVE YOURSELF

No matter who you really are.

PART 3:
HOW TO TAP
INTO THE
MOTHERLODE

CHAPTER 10:

MEDITATION 101

You are never alone or helpless. The force that guides the stars guides you too.
—Shrii Shrii Anandamurti; Indian philosopher, social revolutionary, author, composer

Meditation, otherwise known as sitting still and thinking about nothing, is one of those things that can be just as stupidly simple as it is surprisingly hard. It reminds me of those contests where a bunch of people stand around a brand-new car or truck, and whoever leaves their hands on it the longest gets to take it home. The winner winds up on the front page of her local paper, victorious and sleepy, smiling from behind the wheel of her newly-won ride with a thumbs up for

the camera: "Tarrytown's very own Jill Boender was the proud winner
of the 2012 Chevy Stand Off, held in Green Bay, Wisconsin, this past
weekend. Jill beat out 68 other contestants from around the country
by standing for 173 hours and 9 minutes in the Home Depot parking
lot with her hands placed with unyielding determination on the hood
of what would soon be her new Chevy Silverado. 'I'm so excited I
won,' she said. 'There was some stiff competition, some folks who I
thought would never back down, but I really brought my A-game.'"

With meditation, the simplicity is equally misleading. *That's all I
have to do to connect with Source Energy? Sit there and do nothing? It can't be
that easy.*

Well . . . it is.

And it's not.

Which is why it's called a meditation *practice*.

When you shut up and meditate for even five minutes and start to
really notice the thoughts that are squirreling around in your brain, it's
rather . . . illuminating. If you're like most people, the majority of your
thoughts are about as valuable and interesting as a bunch of two-year
olds fighting over a sippy cup. The goal is to quiet your mind of the
chatter so you can connect to Source Energy and instead listen to your
inner guidance.

I'm going to give you the breakdown on how to meditate, but first
I want to recommend that you start small and work your way up. Try
meditating for five to ten minutes each day at first and add on time as
you get less squirmy.

There's no right way or wrong way to do this, no set amount of
time, no correct things to feel, no rules about how you have to sit or
where you have to do it. All that matters is that you do it if you want
to massively improve your life. It's like drinking lots of water or exer-
cising regularly or not badmouthing other people—you don't *have* to
do it, and the temptation to blow it off is extremely large, but if you

make a habit of it, not only will you start to crave it, but your entire life will change. Because when we meditate, we practice getting into The Vortex and connecting to Source Energy, which automatically:

- Brings us into the present moment

- Raises our frequency

- Opens us up to receive unlimited information and ideas

- Relaxes us

- Relieves stress

- Strengthens our intuition and ability to focus

- Allows us to hear our inner voice more clearly

- Fills us with light and love

- Puts us in a good mood

- Helps us love ourselves

....

Meditating, and being in The Vortex, is like riding the airstream of awesomeness.

....

Here are the extremely short and simple steps of some different ways to meditate:

BASIC MEDITATION

• Sit in a comfortable, cross-legged position on the floor, or in a chair, with your hands on your knees or in your lap.

• Sit up straight and relax your entire face, especially your jaw and your forehead.

• Close your eyes, or, if it helps you focus and not fall asleep, keep them open and gaze softly at a spot on the ground a couple feet in front of you.

• Focus on your breathing. Notice it moving in and out of your body; you don't have to breathe in any special way. Just focus on it.

• Gently release any thoughts that come into your brain and refocus on your breathing. Keep your mind as clear and empty as possible and listen for intuitive hits that may or may not come through.

Tah–dah! That's it.

OPTIONS AND SUGGESTIONS

1. Set a timer. You've got enough distracting thoughts without checking the clock to see how long you've been at it every thirty seconds.

2. Light a candle and focus on it. Sometimes having a place to

rest your eyes can help you get centered and in the Zone. Sit and face a candle that you place on the floor in front of you while you meditate and see if that works for you.

3. Imagine a bright beam of light shooting down from the sky, shining in through the top of your head, running through your entire body, out your bottom and up to the sky again so that it makes a complete circle. I sometimes find this easier to focus on than the ever-popular breath method, plus it fills me up with energy and light and makes me feel more deeply connected to Source Energy.

4. Use a mantra. Sometimes when the squirrels in my head are particularly active, I bring in a mantra to chase them out. I repeat a word or phrase in my mind like "love" or "thank you" or "yes, please" or "om"—something that makes me feel good and is fairly neutral, but you could use a mantra like "meatloaf" I guess if that's your thing.

5. Try and do it first thing in the morning so you're not distracted by whatever the day brings. You'll also be more connected having just woken up from sleeping.

6. If there's something in your life that you're working on or through, you can set an intention/ask for help during your meditation practice. Meditating is about receiving information from The Universe; setting intentions and praying are about sending information out to The Universe. There are two ways you can do this: A) Start with a question, something like, *How do I deal with my pain-in-the-ass teenage son?* And see what, if any, answers download while you meditate, or B) Meditate first, open up the

channel, clear out the chatter, and then ask your question in a space of clarity and connection and see what, if anything, comes to you.

GUIDED MEDITATION

There are countless CDs and DVDs that various hippies and guru types have made over the years to walk you through meditations. I suggest taking the guided route when you're first starting out if you're having trouble wrangling your mind into submission. They make great training wheels and I still use them occasionally, especially if I want to focus on something specific.

There are also guided meditation centers all over the place, and it's really nice every once in a while to meditate in a group— you can really feed off that energy and get the discipline to sit there for an extended period of time. Do a search for meditation centers and ashrams in your area. Sometimes yoga studios hold guided meditations, too.

CHANTING

Chanting is also a great way to get into a meditative state. You can repeat a mantra over and over out loud on your own or, if you prefer to avoid getting busted and very possibly ridiculed, you can do it in a group by attending a Kirtan meditation class. Kirtan meditation involves call-and-response chanting of Sanskrit mantras or devotional songs, and you can attend classes at a yoga studio or meditation center. Also check out Transcendental Meditation instruction, a form that involves repeating mantras and sitting twice a day for around twenty minutes at a time.

I've had some pretty profound experiences while meditating; I've seen the walls melt around me, felt like I was levitating, and have experienced such a state of euphoria that it almost hurt. I've also had extremely un-profound experiences; I've fallen asleep, spent the entire time squirming and thinking about what to make for lunch, and have been totally in The Zone, and then realized I was in The Zone, and thought *Awesome, I'm in The Zone!* Thereby pulling myself out of The Zone.

The important thing is that you keep showing up. Even if you're only in The Zone for one collective minute out of the thirty minutes you've been sitting there, it will eventually start making a notable difference in your life.

I think meditation is even more essential now that we have all this technology at our fingertips and distraction has become a way of life. While I truly believe that we, as a species, are becoming more and more conscious, I'm amazed by how, at the same time, our attention spans are rapidly shrinking. I was playing tennis the other day with someone who got a text, pulled out his phone, and checked it *in the middle of a point*. It's astonishing that we can still speak in full sentences.

Aside from being one of the most powerful tools in our consciousness-raising toolbox, meditation is a much-needed respite from the madness, and will help us from becoming a bunch of scatterbrained ding-dongs as we zoom around our brave, and extremely exciting, new world.

CHAPTER 11:

YOUR BRAIN IS YOUR BITCH

Mind is the master power that molds and makes
And man is Mind and evermore he takes
The tool of Thought and, shaping what he wills
Brings forth a thousand joys, a thousand ills.
He thinks in secret, and it comes to pass:
Environment is but his looking glass.

—James Allen; old-timey author, self-help pontificator

How often do you stop and notice how genius our Universe is? With all its moving parts and mathematical perfection and chemical reactions and food chains and gravity and all the magnificent efficiency and complexity that makes it up? This display of astonishing brilliance didn't just splat down into being-ness by random, dumb luck, it was thought up. Nature is a smoothly running machine, created by a Universal intelligence, where nothing goes to waste; it all has a place and a purpose, and it all works together in its intricately interwoven and compatible way to create the flabbergasting is-ness of it all.

In other words, Source Energy is a smartypants.

As British philosophical writer and self-help pioneer, James Allen, states in the quote that opens this chapter, "Mind is the master power that moulds and makes, -and Man is Mind. . . ."—we are the very thinking substance that was used to create us. Hello?! How major is that?!

This is why positive thinking is all the rage and negative subconscious beliefs are so gnarly and why meditation, and learning to guide your thoughts and love yourself, can change your life.

Our thoughts are the most powerful tools we've got.

I think, therefore, I can create awesomeness. Or horrendousness. But the bottom line is that it's through our thoughts that we create our realities.

It's also why buying into whatever illusion you're living in in the present moment is selling yourself so short if it's anything less than what you truly desire. You created the reality you now exist in with your thoughts, which means you can use the very same power of thought to change it. As Wallace Wattles, author of *The Science of Getting Rich*, so brilliantly states:

To think what you want to think is to think the truth, regardless of appearances.

"To think what you want to think is to think truth"—is that not the best news ever? It doesn't matter what your reality looks like at the moment, because where you desire to be is the truth, the whole truth, and nothing but the truth, and if you fixate your mind on this truth, believe that it is real and already here, and take decisive action, it will manifest itself.

This is where most people dig in their heels and say something like, "I am sitting in my ghetto-ass kitchen eating tuna out of a can with a plastic spoon and you're telling me this isn't the truth? You're saying that the truth is that I'm hanging poolside with the president of the United States of America?" If you truly *desire* to hang poolside with the president of the United States of America, and are hell-bent in your mind and your actions to create it, it's the truth.

Have you ever noticed how a bunch of people can go through the same course, let's say a class on how to start your own coaching business, and they all get the exact same information and tools, but some will come out of there and totally rock it and others will fall flat on their faces? Even if they all have the same desire to succeed, create beautiful marketing materials and *do* similar things, it's the ones with the proper mindsets who will succeed. The ones who kick ass are the ones who can see themselves kicking ass, who truly believe in themselves and what they're selling, who remind themselves how much they want to better people's lives with their coaching, who are excited to get compensated for selling it and have no limiting, subconscious beliefs holding them back. The ones who feel weird or who worry that they're being pushy and annoying or who subconsciously believe that they don't deserve to or can't succeed—they're not gonna do so good.

Your thoughts and beliefs dictate your reality, so if you want to change your reality, you have to change your beliefs. The problem is that most people are rill protective of their beliefs and are usually fairly crotchety should you suggest that perhaps there's another version of the truth. *I'm bad at sales; I have terrible luck; I'm scared of flying; marriages don't last, I have ugly feet, I'm broke . . .* "Are you calling me a liar? Do you see a hot boyfriend on my arm? No you don't, you see a cat on my lap next to my needlepoint project because I stink at relationships—that is the truth and that always has been the truth." And that will be your truth as long as you choose to think it. As long as you feed the beast, it shall live.

••

The moment you have the audacity to start believing in the not-yet seen, your reality will begin to shift.

THE FOLLOWING IS HUGELY IMPORTANT SO PLEASE PAY VERY CLOSE ATTENTION: You have to change your thinking first, and then the evidence appears. Our big mistake is that we do it the other way around. We demand to see the evidence before we believe it to be true.

••

Remember, everything you desire is right here, right now. You just have to shift your perception in order to see it made manifest.

"Okay, fine. I believe that I'm hanging poolside with the President of the United States of America. Now what? Do I just call? Or show up at the White House in my flip-flops with a towel around my neck?" When you take the leap and believe in the not-yet seen, you aren't supposed to know how to make it happen, because if you knew how, you probably would have done it already. This is about radically changing your reality, so the way to go about it is also most likely outside of your present awareness.

....

Your job isn't to know the *how*, it's to know the *what* and to be open to discovering, and receiving, the *how*.

....

Keep your thoughts directed at your goal, do everything that you DO know how to do to make it happen, decide with unwavering determination that it will happen, and be on the lookout for the opportunity.

I had a client who went to Tuscany and looked at a house that was for sale while she was there. At the time, she was a bartender and a poet and could barely scrape together the money to buy a plane ticket to Italy, let alone to buy a Tuscan villa, but she checked it out anyway and completely fell in love with the place. While she instantly knew in her soul that it was her house, she also knew that her bank account had tumbleweeds blowing through it, but she asked the owners to take it off the market anyway because she was going to figure out a way to buy it.

So she flies home, in a stupor, thinking that perhaps she has gone completely insane, but she sticks to her guns and starts asking around for ideas. She is almost immediately buried beneath a pile of warnings from everyone around her: *It's a huge responsibility not to mention all the complications that come with being in another country and last time I checked you don't speak Italian nor are you a citizen nor do you know a single thing about home ownership and considering you can't even afford to get your teeth cleaned how are you planning on paying a mortgage* and yadda, yadda, yadda. Yet she keeps on going, because in spite of all the evidence otherwise, *she believes this is her house.* This is her truth.

Finally someone mentions the idea of pre-renting blocks of time in the house to raise the money to buy it. People could pay for their time a year in advance, she would just need to sell enough blocks of time to pay for the house, and voila! Cut to her discovering this sort of thing is illegal, going back to the drawing board, trying a million other things, discovering that it's actually *not* illegal, then pre-selling enough rental slots and borrowing some money and to make a very long and ups-and-downs-y story short, she's owned the villa for several years and is thinking about buying another.

You have got to get a handle on your thoughts if you want to change your life. As Albert Einstein so aptly noted, "The world as we have created it is a process of our thinking. It cannot be changed without changing our thinking."

Here are some tried-and-true ways to show your brain who's driving the bus:

1. ASK AND IT IS GIVEN

Get quiet, get in The Zone, and get in touch with Source Energy. Clear out the chatter in your brain and create a clean, uncluttered space to impress the thoughts of what you want into the giant thinking substance that is Source Energy. Ask for what you want, send out a nice, clear message in a nice, clear space and begin the manifestation process.

2. ACT AS IF

If you want something badly, even if you don't have any evidence that it's possible for you to attain, believe it is anyway. Fake it until you make it. Do it in spite of yourself. Act as if. If you have an intense, undying desire to hang poolside with the president of the United

States of America, think about the things that a person hanging poolside with the leader of the free world would do. Go pick out the
bathing suit you're going to wear. Think of what you're going to talk
about. Get your photos of your trip to the Grand Canyon together to
show the commander in chief. Get ready for the event. Tell yourself it's
happening. Act like it's happening. Put yourself in situations where you
will meet people who can make this happen. Stay wide open to opportunities that can lead you to your goal. Live, eat, sleep, and breathe
your vision. You may feel like a crazy person, but you won't when
you're playing Marco Polo with the prez.

3. UPGRADE YOUR ENVIRONMENT

If you aspire to have a more up-leveled and inspiring lifestyle than
you presently have, and you're actively visualizing this for yourself, it's
going to be quite a struggle to keep your thoughts large and in charge
if every time you pull up to your rickety-ass home you hear the
Sanford and Son theme song start up in your head. So even though
you're going to be thinking and imagining the change *before* it happens,
do what you can to make some upgrades to where you're at now. Give
the place a paint job and clean it up. Get new furniture or fix up what
you already have. Throw out the clutter, let some air in, hang inspiring
art on the walls. This will not only help to keep your frequency high,
but it will alert The Universe that you're not screwing around, that
you're doing everything you can and are waiting for further instruction
on the *how*.

4. MAKE A VISION BOARD

Our minds think in images: If someone says, *a horse wearing red lipstick,* you instantly create a picture in your mind of a horse wearing red lipstick. Feeding your mind full of images of the things and experiences that you want to manifest—your dream house with the infinity pool in Mexico, rolling around on the beach with your red hot lovah, volunteering to help little kids learn how to read at your local library, laughing your face off surrounded by dear friends—is hugely powerful because your mind sends that image out to Source Energy which begins the process of pulling it in. Cut out pictures of places, people, things, and experiences that you want in your life, paste them onto a board and hang it somewhere where you'll see it all day long. I've seen people have completely insane results with this. They've manifested, down to the tiniest details, the exact home or piece of furniture or place of employment that they put on their board. It's freaky- deaky. And super easy. It's like having a craft day with God. Give it a shot.

5. SURROUND YOURSELF WITH PEOPLE WHO THINK THE WAY YOU WANT TO THINK

When you hang out with whiners, pessimists, tweakers, bleakers, freakers-outers and life-is-so-unfairers, it's an uphill climb to keep yourself in a positive headspace. Stay away from people with tiny minds and tiny thoughts and start hanging out with people who see limitless possibility as the reality. Surround yourself with people who act on their big ideas, who take action on making positive change in the world and who see nothing as out of their reach.

Make a conscious choice to do this. And if you don't know anyone who's got a big fat mind, go out and make some new friends. If you stop at, "there's no one like that around here," that will be the truth and will set the wimpy tone for how you go about trying to manifest everything else into your life. How you do one thing is how you do everything. Get out there and find some people who make you feel like you can leap tall buildings in a single bound. Be clear on whom you want to meet and make a concerted effort to go meet them. Demand of The Universe to connect you with them, think of places where they might hang out or things they would do and insert yourself there. Being around inspired, visionary, enthusiastic people who are living their truths is one of the fastest ways to massively transform your life.

6. LOVE YOURSELF

Unless you have a better idea.

CHAPTER 12:

LEAD WITH YOUR CROTCH

In the beginner's mind there are many possibilities, but in the expert's there are few.
**—Shunryu Suzuki; Japanese Zen monk, author, teacher
also lovingly known as the "Crooked Cucumber"**

I know the big saying is "youth is wasted on the young," but I think, in certain respects anyway, we've really got it going on in our late teens and early twenties. Aside from all the angst and drama and escorts home from the police, we've still got our little kid-like ability to create "just because" still firmly intact, but we've also got this newly-hatched adult ability to make big things happen in our lives. Add to this the fact that we're not yet jaded by a long list of failures, and are still under the vague impression that death is something that happens to other people, we, if you're anything like me, leap into our lives when we're young with an idiotic, yet awesome, disregard for "what-if's."

Admittedly, I remember doing things in the danger department that still have me sleeping with my light on when I think about them now: hanging out in sketchy parts of town with even sketchier people, stowing away on trains, taking enough LSD in one sitting to keep an entire village staring at their hands for hours, hiking off into the desert with no water, no map, and a canteen full of gin and tonics—my first priority being fun, with thoughts of the consequences trailing somewhere, if at all, far off in the distance.

But I also remember diving into my creative pursuits with the same reckless obliviousness and, as a result, getting utterly spectacular and thrilling results. Which is why I find it so odd to hear people say, "If I knew then what I know now, I'm not sure I would have done it." Well thank God you didn't know if that's yer lame-o attitude. You'd be sitting next to a pile of empty beer cans, whining about how you missed out on going for your dreams if you did!

The problem is that once we're older and "wiser," many people trade in living fully in their purpose for more "grown-up" versions of life that range from the merely passable to the full-on sucking. They've bought into this idea that being responsible = not having fun anymore, that waking up feeling excited about life is for the young, and once we're older, we need to trade that in, settle down and be more "realistic."

Yawn.

I'm not talking about being an irresponsible jerk or doing the same things we did when we were younger, but I am talking about continuously living our dreams, no matter what stage of life we're in, instead of settling for mediocrity because we don't believe anything else is available or appropriate.

We only get to be in our bodies for a limited time, why not celebrate the journey instead of merely riding it out until it's over?

We're still allowed to dream, and our dreams are still available to us, but as we move through life, we must make the conscious effort to overcome whatever judgments we have, as well as kick all our fears from past experiences in the head, and participate in our own badassery. Whatever that looks like for us. We must focus on the positive instead of the list of negatives we've collected over time, and keep that focus regardless of what flies in our faces. And one of the best ways to do this is by reconnecting with our inner kids. I know how unacceptably dorky this may sound, but just stay with me here.

Even though you're now most likely turned on by different things than you were as a youngster, you can still learn a lot from how you went about life in the old days. So think back: Was there ever a time where you felt totally in your groove? Where you created and did stuff just because it was fun without worrying about the outcome? Where you couldn't wait to wake up in the morning and go do your thing? This could mean anything from when you were a little kid running around with a maxi pad stuck to your eye pretending to be a pirate to your senior year in high school when you got voted Class Clown for repeatedly charming your way past the ladies in the front office to make fake announcements over the loud speaker to that summer you learned to play the guitar without looking at your hands. When were you most turned on by life (and if you have yet to feel this way, stay tuned . . .) and what can you learn from those experiences?

For me, one of the most exciting and on-purpose times in my life was when I was the singer-guitarist in a band called Crotch. I use the terms "singer," "guitarist," and "band," all very loosely because we in Crotch weren't concerned with things like learning to play our instru-

ments or practicing or any of that snooty musicianship crap. We had
bigger fish to fry, like talking in loud voices about our band and checking ourselves out in plate glass windows as we walked by with guitars
strapped to our backs.

Electric ones.

I started Crotch with this chick from work named Paula who'd
never picked up a guitar in her life either, and who was as incapable of
embracing her feminine side as I was. Paula and I were the kind of
young ladies who prided ourselves on the wattage of our stereo equipment, our firm handshakes, and our ability to drink anyone in the
room under the table.

The testosterone-fueled chip on my shoulder came from a high
school career spent futilely awaiting a timely puberty while standing a
good foot taller than everyone on earth, all the boys at my high school
included. None of them ever asked me out, but I could make them
laugh and kick their asses at basketball, so rather than fail at seducing
them, I simply became one of them.

Paula's issues were more homicidal in nature. She was the kind of
angry found in highly intelligent women who develop the body of a
Playboy bunny by the age of thirteen and are forced to grow up in the
deep, redneck South. Within the first few months of starting the band,
she traded in her long, raven locks for a fire-engine red buzz cut and
covered her arms and back with tattoos of flames and dragons.

We decided that as the tough one, she should play bass while I, the
desperate-for-attention one, would be on guitar, and that my little
brother, Stephen, the malleable one, would play drums. "Only until we
find another drummer," I promised him, as I attempted to plug my guitar into the wrong part of my amp. Stephen has played the drums since
he was five, and is the kind of younger brother every bossy older sister dreams of: talented and endlessly enthusiastic with a very high
threshold for pain.

The great tragedy of Crotch was that underneath our sneers and our bravado, we were two sweet girls who desperately wanted boyfriends. But we had issues—issues that we decided were best worked out while drunk, and sometimes naked, on stage. Paula and I, baffled by our lack of gentlemen callers, chose to express our disappointment by writing and singing songs like *Sew Me Up I've Had Enough* and by yelling things into the microphone between songs that one evening would inspire an audience member to rush the stage holding a chair over his head with intent to beat us with it.

In spite of ourselves, we quickly acquired quite the following. In less than a year's time we also wrote, produced, directed, and starred in a film about the record industry; wrote, directed, and starred in a music video that got on national television; recorded an EP, got a demo deal with Columbia Records, and even learned a couple more chords. And we did it with full-time corporate jobs and no idea what we were doing. It was fun with a capital "F."

•••

There's nothing as unstoppable as a freight train full of fuck-yeah.

•••

If you've ever known what it's like to be in your groove, and are having trouble finding your way right now, think back to your attitude and what your priorities were when you were totally lit up about life, and use them to help give you the clarity and the kick in the rear end you need now.

Here are some nuggets of wisdom I gleaned from the Crotch days that I still find useful:

1. JUST SEE WHAT YOU CAN GET AWAY WITH

Life is r–i–d–i–c–u–l–o–u–s. It so seriously is—we have no freakin' idea what we're even doing here spinning around on this globe in the middle of this solar system with who-the-hell-knows-what out there beyond it. Making a big fat deal out of anything is absurd. It makes much more sense to go after life with a sense of, "Why not?" instead of a furrowed brow. One of the best things I ever did was make my motto "I just wanna see what I can get away with." It takes all the pressure off, puts the punk rock attitude in, and reminds me that life is but a game.

Yes, we have bigger responsibilities and more pressure as adults, but come on folks, I guarantee you there are countless people with waaaaaaaay more to whine about out there than you who are totally kicking ass because they decided to go for it instead of sitting around in the wet pantload of their own excuses. Take a new approach to what you're doing and try this on: *I just wanna see if I can start my own successful business; I just wanna see if I can get myself out of debt and make one hundred thousand dollars more this year; I just wanna see if I can lose a hundred pounds; I just wanna see if I can sell one of my paintings for fifty grand; I just wanna see if I can meet my soul mate.*

Take the pressure off and get back in on the adventure.

2. LOSE TRACK OF TIME

Have you ever been doing something and suddenly realized that hours have gone by without you noticing? What does that for you? And how often during your day does this happen? When you're so lost in what you're doing that you lose all sense of time, you have officially entered the Vortex. You want to get your ass in there as much as possible, so look at your life and figure out how you can make that happen.

First, figure out the things you get lost in in your business and your personal life. Then figure out how you can be doing more of those things more of the time. Hire someone (no excuses) and delegate the tasks you hate doing. Partner up with someone who's good at, and enjoys doing the things you're not that into, so you can be freed up to do more of what you want. If you have to, make massive changes in your business and your personal life to include more time doing what you love. Figure it out. Don't just hand your life over to your circumstances like a little wuss. You can take your life wherever you want it to go, so grab it by its nether regions and make doing the things you love a priority.

3. KEEP BEING THE BEGINNER

One of the best things about starting a band when you have no idea how to play your instrument is that you don't care if you stink because you already know you do. Then once you learn how to play, you get all serious, you become overly critical and hard on yourself and don't let yourself have nearly as much fun anymore. The trick is to let the Beginner live alongside the Expert, instead of pretending you don't know who she is when she tries to sit with you and your new, cooler, more experienced friends in the cafeteria. The Beginner may be an idiot, but she knows how to party, and if you don't let her play with you anymore, things risk getting rather droll around here. So hone your skills; take your craft seriously; learn what you need to learn; invest in yourself; practice your ass off; fall down; get up; keep going; get really really really really good at what you do, but don't lose the fun in the process. Because, like, what's the point of doing all that work then? The only thing you need to do is do the very best you can. Once

you've done that, the only other thing that matters is that you enjoy
yourself.

4. LOVE YOURSELF

And the bluebirds of happiness will be your permanent backup singers.

CHAPTER 13:

GIVE AND LET GIVE

It is one of the beautiful compensations in this life that no one can sincerely try to help another without helping himself.
—Ralph Waldo Emerson; American poet, essayist, visionary, giver

One day while driving somewhere with my family, we stopped off at a store along the way and told my niece, then five years old, that she could get herself a little sumthin'. She came up to the register with a six-pack of orange Tic Tacs and charmed her way into getting the whole thing, instead of being told to put it back and just buy one.

So we get back in the car and I ask her if I can have a pack, my only intent to teach the greedy little piglet a thing or two about sharing. "Of course," she says and hands it over. She then asks, in her itty-bitty five-year-old voice, if my brother and my mom want one too, and hands them over. My niece then takes her remaining three packs and places them on the seat next to her in a pile saying, "And when we get home, this one's for my brother, this one's for my sister, this one's for my mom." Then she sits there, with none left for herself, and smiles, more excited to give them away than she was when she was told she could buy them for herself.

I shot a confused look at my brother, Stephen, her father, and he mouthed back "freak." When Stephen and I were her age, we cherished nothing more than the tortured cries of the other. He set my gerbils free in the backyard. I stole his Halloween candy and ate it, piece by piece, sitting on his chest while he screamed. Who was this saintly creature in the backseat and where did she learn that?

As my niece so clearly understood, giving is one of our greatest joys. It's also one of the most fearless and powerful gestures there is. When we trust that we live in an abundant universe and allow ourselves to give freely, we raise our frequency, strengthen our faith, and feel awesome, thereby putting ourselves in flow and the position to receive abundant amounts in return.

When we're in fear, we hold on to what we've got because we don't trust that there's more. We pinch off the energy, we're scared to share, and we focus on, and create more of, the very thing we're hoping to avoid, which is lack.

We live in a universe of give and receive, breathe and exhale, live and die, suck and awesome. Each side depends on the other, and each is relative to the other—every action has an equal and opposite reaction—so the more you give, the more you receive. And vice versa.

You may be thinking, *that's so not true, I know some bitches who do nothing but take and haven't given a damn thing to anybody, ever,* but receiving has a different energy than selfishly taking, just as smothering has a different energy than giving. Smothering and taking are fear-based and needy, giving and receiving are full of gratitude and surrendering to the flow.

I know someone who has multiple sclerosis who was told by a mentor to give away twenty-nine things for twenty-nine days as part of her cure. She blew it off for a while, but as her condition worsened, she finally decided to give it a try. First, she gave a phone call to a sick friend to see how she was doing. Then she steadily gave away something every day and she almost instantly found herself more joyful and excited. By the fourteenth day she was significantly better physically, her business started booming, and she went on to create a blog that started a movement with tens of thousands of followers who were also giving things away daily. Her blog ultimately led to a *New York Times* best-selling book called *29 Gifts*.

If you want to attract good things and feelings into your life, send awesomeness out to everyone around you. Here are some good ways to get in the give-and-take flow, yo:

1. If you haven't already, pick one or two causes that have real meaning to you and give to them every month. Give however much time or money you can, but do it consistently so it becomes a habit, so it becomes part of who you are. Even five dollars a month counts.

2. Give one of your favorite things in the world away to someone who would totally love it. And if you can, do it without them knowing where it came from.

3. Leave a dollar more than you normally would every time you tip. Or ten.

4. If someone is being snarky, instead of sinking to their level

and being snarky back, raise them up by giving them the love.

5. Smile, compliment, and crack people up as often as possible.

6. Say yes to invitations that you wouldn't normally say yes to because you hate to inconvenience the person offering. Take them up on it. Give them the opportunity to give to you.

7. Stop and feel in your body how great it feels when you give and receive; raise your frequency and expect more good things to come your way.

8. LOVE YOURSELF

And everybody benefits.

CHAPTER 14:

GRATITUDE: THE GATEWAY DRUG TO AWESOMENESS

When you are grateful, fear disappears and abundance appears.
—**Anthony Robbins; author, speaker, motivator, life-changer**

When I was a little kid, my parents made my brothers and sister and I answer the phone in this very formal way, "Jennifer Sincero speaking," as if, between fighting over who got to play with the Big Wheel and stuffing balloons down our pants, we were all running our own private concierge businesses. Their friends would gush on the other end of the phone about what a polite bunch the Sincero kids were, and I thought nothing of it until the day I made my very first phone call to a friend, and, upon hearing her answer, gripped the phone in wide-eyed disbelief. *You get to say "Hello?" Do your parents know?!* It was as unthinkable to me at the time as saying the F-word or sitting down to join my parents for a glass of scotch.

My amazement quickly turned to horror when I realized it wasn't just that one renegade friend who could answer the phone in such a carefree manner, but everyone, and that my parents were clearly playing some big practical joke on us. Our objections were met with the standard, "When you pay your own phone bill you can answer it any way you like." So the years passed, our indignation slowly getting watered down by habit.

I don't remember exactly when the mutiny happened, but eventually we all started answering the phone like normal human beings. I'm going to assume it was around the time of their divorce, when Mom had all four of us mostly to herself, either in, or hovering around, high school, and phone rules got bulldozed in her switch to combat mode.

The demand for manners in general, however, was left firmly standing, and no matter how wild and wasted we got, we always remained those polite Sincero kids: "Can I help you Officer? Thank you, Officer. Yes, sir, that is my marijuana." Not only are the words "please" and "thank you" ingrained in me like the recipe for my Italian father's red sauce or the knowledge that it's not cool to kill people, but being polite just always seemed to be such a no-brainer. Aside from the fact that it makes you feel like a good person, people will usually do what you ask them to do if you're nice about it, and if you're not, they won't. Hello? Which is why it completely baffles me when anyone over the age of five is rude, and especially when they refrain from the thank-you part of the conversation when a gesture is made on their behalf, either by me or other people or The Universe in general.

I don't know about you, but when someone doesn't say thank you after I've hooked them up, it's as glaring an omission to me as if they've shown up without their pants on. And The Universe feels the same way.

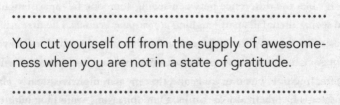

You cut yourself off from the supply of awesomeness when you are not in a state of gratitude.

Having gratitude goes way beyond just having good manners, however. Manners are a form of custom, gratitude is a state of *being*. Anyone can whip out their P's and Q's whether they're feeling it or not, but truly being in a state of gratitude is about having an awareness of, and a deep appreciation for, the many miracles in your life.

Think about how it feels when you get to really thank someone for doing something for you. You feel great for receiving whatever it is you received and for sending thanks out to them, and they feel great for giving you whatever they gave and for being appreciated. Which makes you feel great again. Which makes them feel great again—you could basically spend the rest of your lives passing thank-you notes back and forth. And because it makes you feel good to be in such a state of gratitude, it puts you at a very high frequency and connects you to Source Energy, which puts you in a more powerful state to manifest more good feeling things and experiences into your life.

Conversely, when you show up disappointed or angry or guilty or oblivious instead of being grateful, you're at a lower frequency and thereby less connected to Source Energy and in a less powerful state to manifest good feeling things and experiences into your life.

So that's all fabulous and great, but here's where the whole gratitude thing gets really cool. There are lots of ways to feel good and raise your frequency and get closer to Source Energy, but with gratitude, you're actually expending positive energy by sending out thanks, which makes positive energy reflect back to you—every action has an equal and opposite reaction. This makes the manifesting process even more powerful.

It's like the difference between seeing someone fall apart laughing and seeing them fall apart laughing *at something you said*. The first usually makes you feel as good and laugh as hard as they do, which raises your frequency, but with the second situation, you're not just meeting them at a high frequency, you're *exchanging energy* at a high frequency. Their laughter is like their way of thanking you for saying something hilarious, and it gives off an even more powerful zing and stronger connection.

As Wallace Wattles explains in *The Science of Getting Rich*: "You cannot exercise much power without gratitude; for it is gratitude that keeps you connected with Power."

You are practically powerless without gratitude—thems is some pretty big words, Wattles! When you actively send this grateful energy out, you receive it back, bringing you closer and closer to Source Energy and raising your frequency higher and higher with each exchange until you come to the visceral understanding that you are the same stuff as Source Energy and that you consciously or unconsciously manifested your reality yourself out of the infinite nothingness and everythingness. Gratitude connects you to the truth that you not only have the power to manifest that which you seek, but you *are* the power. Which means, in essence, when you are being grateful to Source Energy you are being grateful to yourself. Which brings it back to the most powerful thing of all: Self- love. Tah dah!

The more consistently you stay in gratitude and focused on that which is good, the stronger your connection to Source Energy is, and the more quickly and effortlessly you'll be able to manifest that which is unseen into your reality.

This is the almighty power of gratitude. But wait, there's more! Gratitude also strengthens your faith.

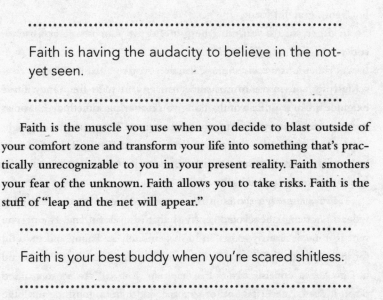

Faith is having the audacity to believe in the not-yet seen.

Faith is the muscle you use when you decide to blast outside of your comfort zone and transform your life into something that's practically unrecognizable to you in your present reality. Faith smothers your fear of the unknown. Faith allows you to take risks. Faith is the stuff of "leap and the net will appear."

Faith is your best buddy when you're scared shitless.

When you are consistently in a state of gratitude, and aware of all the awesomeness that already exists, it, among many other things, makes it much easier for you to believe that there's more awesomeness where that came from, and that this yet-to-be-manifested awesomeness is also available to you. You've received awesomeness before, so of course, you can receive awesomeness again. This is how gratitude strengthens your faith. And having strong faith is a major key in transforming your life.

Which brings me to the grand gratitude finale—if you want to be a real rock star in the manifestation department, get to the point where you have *both* unwavering faith and unwavering gratitude for that which you desire. This is when the real magic happens because *mixing faith with gratitude is the High Holy Moly of Manifesting.*

This takes some Jedi mastery, however, because basically what it entails is not only believing in the not yet manifested (having faith), but being grateful for it.

In other words, you must be grateful for your imaginary friends and your imaginary life. Yep.

As ridiculous as this sounds, I'm sure you're already doing it consciously or unconsciously in some capacity in your life. One simple example from my life would be with finding parking spaces. For as long as I can remember, I've always gotten stellar parking spots, right out front of wherever I'm going. I don't care if I'm trying to park in front of the Pope's house on Easter Sunday, if you don't want to walk, you'll be wantin' to ride with me.

I always approach the hunt for a parking space with the same attitude; a knowing and relaxed certainty that it's a done deal. The perfect spot is mine, it already exists and I'm genuinely so happy and grateful for it. I really truly *believe* this. Then, as always, someone pulls out and in I go. Yet as consistently as this happens, I'm still always so excited when it does. I never take it for granted, and I am a gratitude machine before, during, and after my guaranteed excellent parking adventure.

• •

Being in gratitude for the not-yet manifested informs The Universe that you know that what you desire already exists, and puts you at the right frequency to receive it.

• •

If you want to radically change your life, strengthen your faith that we live in an abundant, benevolent Universe by being grateful for everything you've already manifested and all the good that's hurtling toward you. Be grateful that you have the power to manifest any reality you desire and then leap into the void to go get it.

Trade in your drama about how you can't have what you want for the grateful expectation that miracles will walk into your life, and the more commonplace those miracles will become.

Here are some ways you can practice:

1. THIS IS GOOD BECAUSE . . .

Whenever anything excellent or mediocre or lame or annoying happens to you, meet it with the statement, "This is good because . . . " and fill in the blank. Once you make this a regular practice, you'll see how much easier it is to be in gratitude for much more than you realized.

"This is good that I got a flat tire on my way home from picking my kids up. I've shown them how to deal in an unexpected situation. Plus I got to spend some quality time hanging out in the car with them playing Twenty Questions while waiting for Triple A to show up. Which is how I found out that my daughter was getting picked on in school."

It's important to look for ways to be grateful for *all* that you've manifested, even things that you might label under "No, thanks." If you focus on the negative aspects of the more challenging things in your life, it will just lower your frequency, keep you in pain and resentment, attract more negativity to you, very possibly make you sick, and very definitely make you crabby. If you instead look for ways to be grateful for everything in your life, it not only raises your frequency, but it allows you to grow by opening you up to the lesson.

Yes, sometimes this is a tall order, and there are absolutely situations in life that just full on blow and leaves us standing there wondering what the hell that was all about. Sometimes it takes years (if ever) before we can look back and say, "You know what? I really needed to get my heart broken into a thousand pieces by that jackass. I'm so much happier with the man I ended up marrying."

Finding the good and the lessons in things allows us to move through them and on to new experiences. If you wanna stay stuck in the same place and keep getting spanked with the same lessons over and over, be negative, resentful, and victimized. If you want to get over your issues and rock your life, be grateful, look for the good and learn.

2. WRITE YOUR THANK-YOU NOTES

Every night before you go to bed, review your day and either write down or mentally note ten things you can be grateful for in your life. These can be everything from the beautiful flowers in your garden to the fact that your heart is beating to the hour-long visit from your persnickety neighbor that taught you to be happy that you don't have her life.

Stopping and noticing throughout the day all the things that you can be grateful for is a great way to keep your frequency high at all times. So try and remember to do it all day long, but at the very least, make it part of your evening routine.

3. LOVE YOURSELF

Be grateful for all you are and all that you're becoming.

CHAPTER 15:

FORGIVE OR FESTER

Forgiveness means giving up all hope for a better past.
—**Lily Tomlin; actress, writer, comedienne, absurdist**

When is the last time you physically hurt yourself? What did you do to get the pain to stop? And how long did you wait to do something about it? When we're in physical pain, we're usually extremely proactive about figuring out how to make it go away immediately because, you know, it hurts. Even if we have to go through more pain from pouring a disinfectant that stings on an open wound or suffering through getting stitches, we do it, right away, because we're very focused on our ultimate goal: relief.

When it comes to our emotional pain, however, we're apparently way more game for seeing just how much torture we can endure, wallowing in our guilt, shame, resentment, and self-loathing, sometimes for entire lifetimes. We prolong our misery by holding on to our ill feelings by badmouthing our mother in-laws, fantasizing about pantsing our loudmouth, incompetent bosses in front of a the whole office, unloading fault on other people, and rolling around in our minds the many reasons why our enemies are wrong and the many reasons why we're right.

We relive our worst moments over and over and over instead of letting them go, we pick at the emotional scabs and refuse to let the healing happen and the pain subside. We won't rest until we've made sure someone else feels as badly as they've just made us feel. *If I have to suffer my entire life I will make sure you see how you've wronged me!* We cling to the resentments that take up our brain space, waste our time, spin us out, keep us angry and depressed and very often make us physically sick and sometimes even kill us because . . . um, why?

Lugging around guilt, shame, resentment and self-loathing is The Big Snooze running the show, pitching a fit, demanding to be right and to be seen. Your higher self, on the other hand, could give a crap about what anybody else thinks or does because your higher self is madly in love with you and that's all that matters. Whatever happened, happened. Holding on will not change this fact, it will just keep the negative feelings from the past alive, keep you a prisoner to your pain and lower your frequency.

The moment you decide to forgive and let your negative feelings melt away, you are on the road to freedom.

Forgiveness is all about taking care of you, not the person you need to forgive. It's about putting your desire to feel good before your desire to be right. It's about taking responsibility for your own happiness instead of pretending it's in somebody else's hands. It's about owning your power by giving all your anger, resentment, and hurt the heave-ho.

Holding on to resentment is like taking poison and waiting for your enemies to die.

If you're having issues with someone you care about, explain how you feel without putting the blame on them and *regardless of the outcome*, forgive them. Your talk may bring you closer together or you may discover that you don't want to hang out with them as much or at all, but either way, if you want to be free, you have to let it go.

If you're feeling hurt or resentful toward some A-hole you don't care about, free yourself and let it go instead of stewing on it or getting revenge by sending them a box of rats in the mail. Why do you care if they understand how lame they are or not—what good does that do you? And don't pretend it's because you want them to become a better person. You could care less. You want retribution or an apology or to be acknowledged as right. Get over it. Let it go. The longer you stay attached to being vindicated, the longer they hang around in your consciousness, stinking up your life. Do not fall prey to the false belief that by forgiving someone you're letting them off the hook. Because when you forgive someone you let yourself off the hook.

. . . .

Forgiving isn't about being nice to them, it's about being nice to yourself.

. . . .

Okay, so great, yes, we get it. Now how do you actually let it all go? How do you forgive the stupid bastard?

1. FIND COMPASSION

Finding compassion for yourself or someone else who did something so so so so awful is like pulling a bullet out of your arm: You may kick and scream and hate it at first, but, in the long run, it's the only way to start the real healing.

One of the best tricks for doing this is to imagine the person you're resentful of as a little kid. Think of this little person acting out of fear, doing the best they can to protect themselves and attempting to deal with their own suffering in the only way they know how. People act poorly because they are in pain or confused or both. Understanding this, and imagining the person who you want to behead as a sweet little innocent child with big puppy dog eyes, will help you find compassion for them, which is the key to forgiveness. And same goes for anything you feel you need to forgive yourself about. You too are just a little bunny trying to work it all out. Find compassion for your sweet little, sippy cup self and let it all go.

2. ERASE THE OTHER PERSON FROM THE EQUATION

Imagine you've got two employees who don't show up for work on the same day, leaving you to handle everything yourself the morning before a huge presentation. One of them blows you off because she's hung over and just couldn't deal, but the other found out that her beloved mother suddenly died and had to run off to the airport, forgetting to call you in her emotional haze.

Same exact result—you're ditched and left to do all the work yourself—two totally different ways to react. Which means . . . . . you have a choice! One choice puts you at risk of busting an artery out of rage, the other opens your heart.

Another option is to picture yourself hanging out in your brand new boat and an empty boat floats up and bangs into you, leaving a scratch. If there's nobody in the boat, there's nobody to get mad at and you deal with the situation in a much calmer, inquisitive way. If there's some moron driving that other boat who bangs into you because they're checking a text, however, you deal with it by going crazy and calling them a bunch of names related to genitalia. Again, same exact situation—you get a scratch on your boat—two different ways to react.

When someone does something awful to you, take that person out of the equation so you can open yourself up to have a more pleasant, and productive, reaction (and life). It's not about them anyway, it's about you. If you have nobody to be angry at, it's hard to be angry. Instead, it opens the incident up for questioning. Why did this happen? How was I involved? Why did I attract this to myself? How can I grow from this? How can I find compassion for everyone involved? When you're consumed by resentment, the lesson can't get through all your inner, and outer, screaming and yelling. Do yourself a favor and use irritating situations and people as opportunities for growth, not pain.

3. DECIDE YOU'D RATHER BE HAPPY THAN RIGHT

Sometimes the road to freedom lies in deciding you'd rather be happy than right. Yes, your idiot friend should have paid the parking ticket she got when she borrowed your car or your brother shouldn't have shaved your dog while he was house sitting for you, but if they don't see it that way, instead of spinning out on it for days, wouldn't it feel so much better to just let it go? Is it really worth lugging around all those foul feelings just so you can be right? Think to yourself, "What do I have to do or not do, or think or not think, right now, to be happy?" And if the answer is "let the jackass think he's right," then so be it.

4. LOOK AT IT FROM ALL ANGLES

It's important to remember that everyone is living in their own self-created illusion, and that you have no idea what they're acting out or where they're coming from, so just because you think something is totally not okay, in their illusion, it could be fine and *your* way could be totally not okay. Look at it from another perspective, loosen your stranglehold on it being *my way or the highway*, let some air in, and you may be surprised how quickly resentment flies out the window.

For example, you send your good friend a text about a dinner party you're having and invite them to come. She sends you a text back saying she can't make it because it's her birthday. You text her back an apology and sad face. You hear nothing back. So you text her "happy birthday!" You still hear nothing back so you proceed to spin out. You go from feeling awful for hurting her feelings to wondering what kind of idiot adult still cares that much about her stupid birthday to thinking how much you'll have to spend on a present to relieve your guilt. Meanwhile, she accidentally dropped her phone in the toilet bowl after her last text to you.

By being inquisitive about, instead of a slave to, your reactions to other people, you get the double whammy bonus of not only setting yourself up to forgive them much more easily (because you realize that it's really about you, not them), but you receive the great gift of being enlightened to some of your own not-so-special traits so you can grow and learn from them (much more on all this in Chapter 21: Millions of Mirrors).

In her brilliant book (I mean it, go get it), *Loving What Is: Four*

Questions That Can Change Your Life, Byron Katie says, "We don't attach to people or things, we attach to uninvestigated concepts that we believe to be true in the moment." For example, in the scenario above, instead of attaching to the "truth" that this person isn't answering your texts because they're upset, all you need to do is ask yourself, "Why am I freaking out over something that I have no proof is even true?" or "How would I feel if I didn't just assume that my friend is mad at me?" You could literally be one question away from being happy in any otherwise upsetting situation.

5. HAVE A TOTAL SHITFIT

Go somewhere alone and far away from other people and beat the hell out of a pillow or a mattress or some other soft, inanimate object that won't hurt your fist or punch you back. Scream and yell about what a selfish little pig this other person is and go for it 100 percent until you're exhausted or someone calls the cops on you. Get it out of your system, totally and completely, and then let it go.

6. REMEMBER THAT YOU WON'T EVEN REMEMBER THIS

Try and think about someone who had you totally freaking out and all pissed off three years ago. Can you even come up with someone? If you can, can you get all worked up about them now? Whatever or whomever you're needing to forgive in this moment will most likely be a mere blip not very long from now (depending on the severity of the situation, of course). So why make a huge drama out of it if you're only going to forget all about it one day? See it as the future non-event that it is and start forgiving and forgetting right away.

When it comes to forgiveness, what you actually have to DO is not hard. It's like quitting smoking—you actually do less than you do when you smoke. You don't have to go to the store to buy cigarettes, you don't have to open the pack, light one up, find an ashtray, etc. All you have to do is stop. All the work is in letting go of your self-created attachment to cigarettes.

Same with forgiveness. All you have to do is let go of your self-created attachment to this other person or belief.

7. FUGGETABOUTIT

Once you've truly forgiven someone, wipe the slate clean. So often we form judgments about people and then, no matter what they do, we see them through the lens of that judgment. Which means we're just waiting for them to piss us off again. Which means we're still in the Forgiveness-lite stage; we're pretending we're cool but we're really still holding on to some resentment. Release all expectations, let everyone off the hook, treat people as a blank slate over and over again, expect only the best from them regardless of what they've done in the past and you may be surprised. What you focus on, you create more of, and if you keep expecting people to annoy you they will not let you down. Focus on their finer points and encourage their good behavior if you want to create more of it.

8. LOVE YOURSELF

You deserve it.

CHAPTER 16:

LOOSEN YOUR BONE, WILMA

You don't paddle against the current, you paddle with it.
And if you get good at it, you throw away the oars.
— **Kris Kristofferson; singer, songwriter, actor, Rhodes**
scholar, still super hot for an old guy

Several years ago I went on a life-changing trip to India. In case you haven't witnessed it yourself, India is heaving with life, a swarming blur of vibrant colors, honking cars, wandering cows, packed trains, endless slums, elaborate palaces, ancient temples, and sweet smelling incense. It's literally full to the brim with humanity, chatting and chanting, and sitting on top of you while you struggle for space on an overbooked train. Your only options are 1.) Go with the flow and get to know your neighbor or 2.) Grow a big, fat stress-related tumor. The thing that made perhaps the biggest impression on me there was how nearly everyone I met went for option number one.

In India, some people will spoon you on a bus if you fall asleep next to them, roll down their windows to chat with you in a traffic jam, stare unblinkingly at your non-Indian-ness, help you if you're lost, insist you get in their family photos at historical monuments, invite you in for tea, burp, fart, and laugh in your face—it's totally annoying. And sweet. And makes me think they clearly know something important that I've long forgotten (and that I suspect most of the world has forgotten, too). I didn't have to darken the doorway of an ashram or stick a red dot on my forehead or partake in any of the other thousands of spiritual options the country is famous for offering—who needs them? As far as I'm concerned, you can learn pretty much everything you need to know about spirituality and life by taking a twelve-hour bus ride through India during wedding season.

When I bought my ticket on the Super Deluxe Express bus to Delhi from Agra, home of the Taj Mahal, I was told I was paying a wise four hundred rupees extra for the luxury of a five-hour nonstop ride, as opposed to the ten hours and countless stops of the local bus. I was so extremely exhausted from the three sleepless days I'd spent whooping it up at a camel festival in the desert that the thought of hunkering down on the Super Deluxe and sleeping all the way to Delhi sounded good to me. But what I got instead was a seat next to Mr. Friendly, a middle-aged man who spoke three words of English, and who insisted on chatting me up even though I was doing what I thought was a very convincing job of fake sleeping, and a very real job of having no freakin' idea what he was saying.

The bus left an hour late due to massive confusion and overbooking and took almost two hours to get out of town thanks to the fact that it was November, peak wedding season. Weddings in India traditionally involve a ceremony that lasts for days, stretches for miles, welcomes anyone caught in the crossfire and includes a parade through the streets complete with horses, marching band, explosives, a car with a loudspeaker blaring Indian music and important wedding announcements, and a bunch of guys carrying what look like table lamps on their heads. My bus ended up getting trapped in wedding festivities pretty much every ten minutes, which meant that everyone on the bus, every time we stopped, skipped off to join the party.

When we finally did get out of town, we kept pulling over to let random people on and off (in the middle of nowhere), have some tea, a smoke, a chat, maybe light a fire in the brush in a ditch or strap giant burlap sacks full of something large and bulbous to the roof. At some point this guy got on who was standing by the side of the road in the darkness. We scooped him up without coming to a full stop and he took his place at the front of the bus, standing right next to my seat, and immediately began hollering at everyone in Hindi. My bus mates responded by cheering, chanting, and sitting in silence, while I responded by seeing if I couldn't find another seat farther away from his mouth. I got up and joined the group of people sitting on rickety benches around the bus driver who was in this "room" behind a wall of glass. The people huddling around him made room for me and suddenly I felt like I was watching an action movie on a screen the size of a giant bus windshield. We were careening through the narrow dirt streets of tiny villages, Bollywood music crackling over the radio, while people, goats, and monkeys leaped out of the way, slowing down only for the almighty, holy cow. Then all of a sudden, in some tiny nowhere village, he pulls over yet again. More chai perhaps? Maybe he's going to go visit a friend? Has to pee? Wants to take a walk for an hour while we all sit there? The driver waves for me to follow and gets off, as does everyone on the bus. It turns out that Mr. Yell in My Ear was some sort of holy man who was just warming up the crowd for a tour of the temples in this small, gorgeous village called Vrindavan. It is, I learned, the place where Krishna met his wife Radha and where they built hundreds of temples in their honor.

So, for the next two hours I found myself wandering through countless temples, gaily tossing flowers onto shrines, holding hands and skipping in a circle around a statue of Krishna, solemnly chanting, praying and clapping, and all I could think was how homicidal a bus of New Yorkers on the express bus from New York to DC would be in a similar situation. Meanwhile, not one person on the bus was expecting this, and not one person complained, even though when we finally got back on the bus it was well past the time we were supposed to be arriving in Delhi and we were still a good five hours away. Instead, they all thanked, and tipped, the holy man and spent the rest of the ride merrily chatting away with one another. After that we stopped at a roadside restaurant for dinner, then another pee break, then I was waking up the family I was staying with in Delhi at 3 a.m. They, of course, acted like it was the middle of the afternoon and insisted I share a cup of tea.

Here's what India taught me about tapping into the Mother Lode:

- Talk to strangers, we're all family on this planet.

- Expect, and enjoy, the unexpected.

- Find the humor.

- Join the party.

- Live in the moment.

- Time spent enjoying yourself is never time wasted.

- Share your space.

- Loosen your bone, Wilma.

LOVE YOURSELF

And life becomes a party.

PART 4:

HOW TO GET OVER YOUR B.S. ALREADY

CHAPTER 17:

IT'S SO EASY ONCE YOU FIGURE OUT IT ISN'T HARD

Reality is merely an illusion, albeit a very persistent one.
—Albert Einstein; scientist, awesomist

I was hanging out in my sunny California home one morning, reading the newspaper with the doors flung open and the stereo blasting, when all of a sudden a bird came tearing into my living room. He was flapping around like a maniac, flying into lamps and plants, spreading leaves, feathers, poop, and panic all over the place.

In an attempt to escape, he kept slamming himself into the window while I feebly chased him around with a flip-flop, trying to guide him back toward the open door. It was awful to watch—the poor guy was all panting and wild-eyed, his little birdy heart no doubt about to explode with fear while he threw himself over and over again into the glass at full speed.

I finally managed to escort him outside to freedom, and then spent a very bothered few minutes calming my own little-birdy heart while I revisited the scene of the accident. I imagined his confusion and frustration: "I can see the sky! It's right there! If I fly hard and fast enough I know I can reach it!"

It made me think of the way so many of us live our lives. We can see what we want, and nearly kill ourselves trying to get it in a way that's not working. Meanwhile, if we just stopped, got quiet for a minute or two, and looked at things a little differently, we'd notice the door to what we want being held open for us by the nice lady in the bathrobe across the room. Then all we'd have to do is fly through it.

Oh, the drama we create for ourselves!

We're so deeply wrapped up in our stories—*I don't have the money, I'm not good enough, I can't quit my job, I'm lazy, I have bad hair*—trudging through life with our heads down, clinging to our false beliefs like lifeboats full of doo-doo, that we prevent ourselves from seeing the literally infinite sea of possibilities and opportunities surrounding us at every single moment.

Have you ever walked down a street that you've walked down a million times and suddenly noticed a house or a tree or a mailbox or something else totally obvious and in-your-face that you've never noticed before? Or have you ever suddenly become aware of the eye color of someone you've known for years? Or have you ever looked at your mother and thought, *I was inside of that woman once!?* All this stuff didn't suddenly appear and then you noticed it, it was there all along, you just weren't experiencing it because your focus was directed somewhere else.

Here's a cool exercise: Right now, look around wherever you are and count the number of things you see that are red. Take about a minute and count them all. Now stop, look back at this page without taking your eyes off of it, and try to think of everything around you that's yellow. There's probably a ton of yellow, but you didn't see it because you were looking for red.

••

What you choose to focus on becomes your reality.

••

And that's just an example of what we're not noticing that we can *see*. There's also an infinite amount of emotions and thoughts and beliefs and interpretations and sounds and dreams and opportunities and smells and points of view and ways to feel good and responses and nonresponses and things to say and ways to help. YET, because we're so set in our ways and committed to our stories about who we are and what our reality looks like, we only scratch the very surface of all that's available to us every single moment. Meanwhile, we're totally surrounded by countless awesome versions of reality, and they're all just hanging around like a bunch of shy teenage girls at the prom, leaning against the walls, waiting for us to ask them to dance.

As the poet William Blake so eloquently stated: "If the doors of perception were cleansed, everything would appear to man as it is, infinite."

So . . . why would you create anything that's not totally awesome? I mean, we're only talking about your *life* here. If you chose to get over all your reasons why the money you so desire is evil or your identity as someone who's scared of intimacy or your attachment to a plethora of other excuses that you perceive to be very serious and real when they're really probably kind of cute and ridiculous—you could literally create any reality you want.

Whenever I become impressed by a particularly creative array of new excuses I've come up with, or start to organize an elaborate pity party for myself, I turn to Ray Charles. I don't often listen to his music, but I always think about Ray when I need a kick in the buttinski. He was a broke, blind, minority who was orphaned by the age of fifteen and raised in the "colored part of town" in a time when slavery wasn't all that distant of a memory, and he went on to become one of the most influential and successful American musicians of all time. Basically, he wasted no time on excuses.

Any little woe-is-me-ism that I try to hold up against Ray instantly wilts into the sniveling little "nice try" that it is, and I'm forced to look upon my life, and my excuses, with a new perspective. *Really? You're really going to let that stop you?*

All you have to do is make the choice to let go of everything you're so attached to that's not serving you and manifest the reality that you want. Life is an illusion created by your perception, and it can be changed the moment you choose to change it.

....

Our entire experience on this planet is determined by how we choose to perceive our reality.

....

I know. As if. It can't be that easy. If it was that simple, how could I possibly have spent all this time banging my head against the glass wall of my own self-created ho-hummery?

But before you get into a bad mood about it, remember: All this stumbling around in the realities we pretend to be stuck in is very valuable because it allows us to grow and learn and evolve—rough seas make better sailors—but you get to choose how long you want to stay in school and work on the same issues over and over and over. Your graduation cap and gown are cleaned and pressed and waiting for you whenever you want to put them on, all you have to do is let go of your present story and rewrite a new one that fits who you truly are.

If you want to join the party and shift your perspective, do what I say in this book (and really DO it, don't just half-ass it. And while you're at it, believe it too). Study the Resources I suggest in the back of this book and on my website. Commit to releasing your attachment to low-frequency thoughts and experiences, trust that the Universe loves the crap out of you, kick fear in the face, and head bravely into the unknown.

Also, do the following:

1. BECOME AWARE OF WHAT YOUR STORIES ARE

We call these "stories" because they are just that. They are not the truth. And they can be rewritten. You're the author of your own life—not your parents, not society, not your partner, not your friends, not the bullies who called you Fatzilla in junior high—and the sooner you decide to write yourself a better script, the sooner you get to live a more awesome life.

Before you can let go of your stories, get clear on what they are. Listen to what you say and what you think about and start busting yourself in your own lies. We get so used to, and so identify with, our broken records that we don't even notice they exist or that they're not even real. And yet we'll fight to the death to uphold their nontruths!

Listen specifically for sentences that begin with:

I always . . .

I never . . .

I can't . . .

I should . . .

I suck at . . .

I wish . . .

I want (as opposed to *I will* and *I am*) . . .

I don't have . . .

One day . . .

I'm trying to . . .

Sad-sack Jane, the lawyer, says she should keep her miserable job at the prestigious firm because she'll never find one that she likes that pays as well. *Really? Is that why nobody on earth, anywhere, is doing a job that they love and making even more money than you make, Jane?*

Lonely-hearted Sally always says she can't find a good, single man because there aren't any left out there. *Really Sally? All the good, single men were hunted down and killed so no matter how many dates you go on or how many times you put on sexy high heels and hang around at Home Depot, you'll never bump into one? Was the awesome guy your friend Deb just met the lone survivor of the good guy genocide?*

Broke-ass Joe, the personal trainer, always talks about how he can't make any money and how there are no high-paying clients out there. *Really Joe? Not any? Anywhere? Then how is it that other personal trainers have more high-paying clients than they can handle? And that some even created energy drinks and work-out products with their pictures on them and are raking it in on QVC?*

Another good place to catch yourself in a story is by looking at the areas in your life that are sagging. If you're constantly angry, maybe your story is, "Nobody understands me." If you're always overweight, maybe your story is, "I have no self-discipline." If you're uninvited from

Thanksgiving dinner because you wouldn't let anyone else talk at the last three family gatherings, maybe your story is, "Nobody pays any attention to me."

Remember, as Wallace Wattles said: *To think what you want to think is to think the truth, regardless of appearances.* Instead of pretending to be stuck in these lame-o realities, use your power of thought to change your attitude and change your life.

Start paying attention: What are your favorite, self-sabotaging stories? What do you hear yourself think and say over and over again that has become who you are (or rather who you think you are)? Bust yourself in your own tired old broken records right now so you can set about rewriting your stories and create the kind of life you love.

2. BECOME AWARE OF WHAT YOU'RE GAINING FROM YOUR STORIES

We pretty much don't ever do anything that we don't benefit from in some way, be it in a healthy way or an unhealthy way. If you're perpetuating something dismal in your life because of some dopey story, there's definitely something about it that you're getting off on.

Let's say, for example, that your story is that you're depressed. Chances are pretty good that even though it feels awful, when you feel awful you don't have to work hard or do the laundry or go to the gym. It also feels very familiar and cozy and comfortable. It gets you attention. People come in and check on you and sometimes bring food. It gives you something to talk about. It allows you to not try too hard or move forward and face possible failure. It lets you drink beer for breakfast.

Let's say your story is that you can't make money. By staying broke, you get to be right. You get to be a victim, which makes you dependent on other people and gets you attention. Other people will offer to pay. You don't have to take responsibility. You get to give up before you start and avoid possible failure. If things in your life fall far below the mediocre scale, you get to blame other people and circumstances instead of taking risks to change it because you can't afford to take risks.

Let's say your story is that you stink at relationships. You get your freedom. You don't have to commit and can keep looking for the greener grass on the other side. You don't have to risk getting hurt by being vulnerable. You get to complain about always being single and get sympathy. You get the whole bed to yourself, never have to compromise, and don't have to shave unless it's summer.

We don't realize it, but we're making the perks we get from perpetuating our stories more important than getting the things we really want because it's familiar territory, it's what we're comfy with and we're scared to let it go. If we've been depressed or victimized or whatever since childhood, we trick ourselves into believing that it's really who we *are* as adults in order to continue reaping "the rewards." It's how we survived as kids, but it doesn't serve us anymore so we need to get rid of it or we'll just keep creating more of it.

For example, let's say you grew up with a violent alcoholic father, and your way to protect yourself from being the target of his rage was to never speak up, to never let yourself or your wants and wishes be visible. Cut to you as an adult who never speaks your truth or who never stands up for yourself. You're still reaping the false rewards, you're playing it safe, not risking getting hurt or yelled at, but this behavior is backfiring on you because by hiding and not taking a stand for yourself, you're living a life that totally makes you want to roll over and go back to sleep every morning instead of getting up and facing your day.

Once you identify the false benefits you're reaping from holding onto your stories, you can start the process of letting them go and replace them with new empowered ones that serve the adult you.

3. GET RID OF YOUR STORIES

Once you know what the beast looks like, you can slay it. Take your list of "can'ts" and "shoulds" and "I nevers," etc., and write stream of consciousness in a journal (see example below), and really feel in your body what you're getting from these old limiting beliefs such as: "I feel special, I feel safe, I get to live with my parents and never get a job," etc. Make a list of these false rewards. Really push yourself to get them all on to the page. Then feel the attention the specialness or the comfort or the safety or whatever your trip is and really become clear on it. Catch yourself fully in the act and feel it all the way through.

Now look at your list of false rewards for what they really are: scared little parts of yourself acting out. Thank them for trying to protect you and for keeping you company, but tell them it's time to run along now.

Then, replace the feelings you got from these false rewards with the feelings of joy and power and excitement that stepping into who you truly are and who you're now becoming will bring.

Imagine that childish version of yourself leaving your body and the powerful adult stepping in. Breathe in the adult; breathe out the kid and the old story. It's like finally taking the keys to the Ferrari back from the seven-year-old version of yourself who's been driving it all this time, nearly getting you killed. See yourself as the adult stepping in to take your place behind the wheel.

Keep envisioning (or writing down) what it looks and feels like to have the real, adult you replace your old childhood story. Feel it. Get excited by it. Then make the decision that you're ready to change and take positive action in the direction you want to go.

For example, let's say that lonely-hearted Sally finally got fed up enough to get mighty real with herself and face her issues around relationships. She'd start by getting clear on what her stories are:

I can't meet a man because there aren't any good ones left.

I suck at flirting.

I never know what to say to men.

I'm not attractive to men. Not the good ones anyway.

I scare men away.

I don't trust men.

I don't believe there really is anyone out there for me.

Once she's got her list (which could easily go on for pages, BTW, but for the sake of example, and because I'd like to leave the house today, we'll stick with these), Sally can stream of consciousness journal about the false rewards she's getting. And by stream of consciousness I mean just let it flow, don't edit or overthink it too much, just write. In Sally's case, her journaling could look like:

By saying there aren't any good men out there I don't have to take responsibility for why I'm not meeting any. I get to feel victimized and right for staying single. I get to prove how lame men are by never being with a good one. My pain of feeling unworthy and my mistrust of men get proven right when I stay single. I feel like I know what I'm doing and in control by not letting anyone get close to me. I feel free. I feel safe. I feel special because I get attention for breaking the rules.

Again, this could go on for pages but you get the idea.

Once she's gotten all her false rewards on the page, Sally can then focus on them, feel them all the way through, thank them for trying to protect her (we don't want to turn this into a self-loathing exercise please) and release them by replacing them with new, powerful stories.

She can literally take each one and replace it with a new truth. For example:

By saying there aren't any good men out there I don't have to take responsibility for why I'm not meeting any.

Then becomes:

The world is filled with awesome, loving men, and I am fully capable of, and so excited to find me a good one.

I get to feel victimized and right for staying single.

Then becomes:

I am powerful and in control of my life. I choose to love and be loved.

I get to prove how lame men are by never being with a good one.

Then becomes:

I love and trust men and am so thrilled to be with an awesome guy who makes me giddy with happiness.

These new stories become her new truth, and in order to make them stick, she focuses on them, breathes them in and feels how happy they make her feel. These stories are her new affirmations (remember those?) that she will not only write down and repeat and bombard herself with over and over and over, but that she will instantly replace her old stories with if they should fly out of her mouth or into her mind out of habit.

Let's review, shall we?

1. List off your old stories that you've gotten into the habit of thinking and saying.

2. Journal about the false rewards you get from them.

3. Feel into these false rewards, thank them for their help, and decide to let them go.

4. Take each false reward and write a new, powerful story to replace it with.

5. Repeat this new story, or affirmation, over and over and over until it becomes your truth.

6. Behold your awesome new life.

Nothing in this world is permanent, including our stories. Yet we try to hold on to them for false security, which ultimately leads to sorrow and loss. Be willing to let go. Keep reinventing your story as you continue to grow.

4. GET A MOVE ON

Once you've gotten clear on your story and have done the energy work above, take action. If you were once depressed but have decided to let it go, stop listening to melancholy music, stop talking about how lousy you feel, stop pretending that putting on your bathrobe counts as getting dressed, etc. Instead, focus on the good and do the things you love to do— make an effort instead of collapsing into the familiar feeling of being depressed.

Realize that you've gotten into habits with these things and switch them around. Behave the way a person who isn't depressed behaves. Dress how they dress, hang out with the kinds of people they hang out with, speak the way they speak, do the things they do. Really sink into the understanding that you can have what you want. This won't work if you just pretend. You can't be like, "Okay, I'm going out on a date, I'm telling myself I am going to have a great time but I know it's going to be hideous because it's always hideous but I'm having a good attitude about it."

....

Going out into the world and trying, yet still deep-down believing that you're ruled by your past circumstances, is like forgiving someone but still hoping they sit in something wet.

....

5. GET OUT OF YOUR ROUTINE

Talk to strangers, wear something different, go to a new grocery store, make dinner for someone who you want to get to know better, change toothpastes, go to a movie at 2 p.m. on a Wednesday, learn three new jokes, walk taller, notice five awesome things you've never noticed about your home, your beliefs, your mother, your face. Do things that pull you out of your routine and you'll be amazed by the new realities that were there all along that suddenly presents themselves.

6. SIDESTEP THE SPIRAL

There's also the ever-popular Spiral Into Darkness where you begin by being sad that your dog died then realize that not only are you now dogless, but you're still single and you will always be single because everyone, including your dog, leaves you, which probably wouldn't be the case if you didn't have such fat thighs or weren't so overshadowed by your gorgeous sister who is pretty much the main reason you've had no self-confidence your entire life and wah wah wah.

Feel sad, but don't blow it up into some huge drama. If something negative happens in your life, feel it, learn from it, let it go and get back to focusing on the life you're excited to live.

7. LOVE YOURSELF

More than you love your drama.

CHAPTER 18:

PROCRASTINATION, PERFECTION, AND A POLISH BEER GARDEN

In order to kick ass you must first lift up your foot.
—Jen Sincero; author, coach, self-quoter

One of my first jobs out of college was production coordinator for the Ethnic Folk Arts Festival, which was put on by a little nonprofit group in New York City. I heard about the position opening up from a friend, and decided I had to have the job even though I'd never produced a thing in my life and find folk art to be fairly yawnable. It looked like fun anyway—they worked out of a funky loft in Tribeca, knew a lot

about music, brought their dogs to work, and the festival I'd be working on gathered musicians, dancers, and artists from around the globe
and brought them together in a Polish beer garden in Queens for a big
fat party. Which meant men in skirts and free sausage and beer.

So I put together a résumé that listed such achievements as: produced plays in college (demanded my friends show up to watch my
boyfriend act); started several organizations in high school (started a
sledding team that had no competition and only one meeting where we
spent most of our time figuring out how to score some beer); worked at
my college radio station (hung around while my friend DJed). Then I
got all dressed up in some business casuals that I borrowed from my
mom that didn't fit and marched off to my interview. A couple of hours
later, me and my big mouth had a new job.

That night I laid awake in wide-eyed horror. My God, what have I
done? I'm a monster! These sweet, big-hearted, sandal-wearing people
just handed me a coffee can full of money that they spent an entire year
collecting for this festival, and I'm the lying fathead who's gonna blow it.

I thought about turning myself in, but, unwilling to turn down a
good party, went for it instead and wound up working harder for them
than I had ever worked in my life. I decided that I'd rise to the occasion, that I would do whatever it took to make this the best damn
festival that that Polish beer garden had ever seen, and I pulled if off
with flying colors if I do say so myself.

I got all twenty-seven of my unemployed friends to hand out fliers
and take tickets in exchange for the aforementioned free sausage and
beer, herded the unruly polka dancers into their places on time, got the
latke vendors set up, and saw to it that the bagpipe parade went off
without a hitch.

If there's something you really want, I'm not (necessarily) saying
you should lie to get it, but I am saying you're probably lying to yourself if you're not going after it.

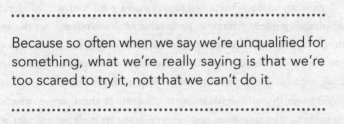

Because so often when we say we're unqualified for something, what we're really saying is that we're too scared to try it, not that we can't do it.

Most of the time it's not lack of experience that's holding us back, but rather the lack of determination to do what we need to do to be successful.

We put so much energy into coming up with excuses why we can't be, do, or have the things we want, and designing the perfect distractions to keep us from our dreams—imagine how far we'd get if we just shut up and used all that energy to go for it instead?

Here's the good news:

1. We all know way more than we give ourselves credit for knowing.

2. We are drawn to things we're naturally good at (which counts more than having a graduate degree in the subject, BTW).

3. There's no better teacher than necessity.

4. Passion trumps fear.

In hindsight, I realized that I was more qualified for that job than I thought. I'm a big sister, which means I'm naturally bossy. I love throwing parties, and I can talk to anyone, even seventy-six-year-old Russian men who don't speak English and are freaking out because they can't find their tights.

I went on to do many more things that I was "unqualified" for, but I also wasted plenty of time pretending I wasn't ready to do some other things I really wanted to do. And, shockingly, the times I jumped in and went for it were way more fun than the than the times I spent sitting around "getting ready," and doing nothing, instead.

Whether it's an online dating profile you're not ready to post or a trip you want to take after you lose ten pounds or a business you want to start as soon as you save enough money . . . just start. Now. Do whatever it takes. You could get run over by the ice-cream man tomorrow.

One time I spent an entire month preparing my office to write a book. I got just the right chair, put the desk in the perfect place by the window, organized all the materials I needed and then reorganized them—three times—cleaned the place until you could perform surgery on the floor, and then proceeded to write the entire thing at my kitchen table.

•••

Procrastination is one of the most popular forms of self-sabotage because it's really easy.

•••

There are so many fun things you can do in order to procrastinate, and there's no lack of other people who are totally psyched to procrastinate with you.

And while it can be super fun in the moment, eventually the naughtiness buzz wears off and you're sitting there a few years later, feeling like a loser, wondering why the hell you still haven't gotten your act together. And why other people you know are getting big fat promotions at their jobs or taking trips around the world or talking about the latest orphanage they've opened in Cambodia on NPR.

If you're serious about changing your life, you'll find a way. If you're not, you'll find an excuse.

In the interest of getting you where you want to go in this lifetime, here are some tried-and-true tips to help you stop procrastinating:

1. REMEMBER THAT DONE IS BETTER THAN PERFECT

Just get the damn website up already or send out the mailer or make the sales calls or book the gig even though you're not totally ready yet. Nobody else cares or will probably even notice that everything isn't 100 percent perfect—and, quite honestly, nothing ever will be 100 percent perfect anyway so you might as well start now. There's no better way to get things done than to already be rolling along—momentum is a wonderful thing, not to mention highly underrated, so get off your ass and get started. NOW!

2. NOTICE WHERE YOU STOP

When you're working on whatever you're working on, or whatever you're pretending to work on, where exactly do you stop? Is it when you have to do the research? Make the scary phone calls? Figure out how to raise the money? Right after you start? When you have to commit? When it starts getting good? Right before it takes off? Before you even get out of bed?

If you can pinpoint the precise moment that you say, "Screw it—

I'm outta here!" you can prepare yourself for hitting the oil slick by hiring coaches or assistants or psyching yourself up or delegating that particular part of it out, or removing known distractions.

For example, let's say you discover that every time you sit down to make calls to try and book yourself a speaking gig, you mysteriously find yourself pulled into Facebook for hours, turn off the Internet, or go someplace to make your calls where you can't get online. Like a park. Or your car. Or Antarctica. And then decide that you have to make five calls before you can check back in and see if anyone commented on the picture you posted of your cat eating a potato chip.

3. MAKE A BET WITH SOMEONE MEAN

A good way to make yourself accountable is to make a bet with someone who will hold you to it. They must have no mercy—they can't coddle you or "understand that you tried your best." You want the kind of person who will make you feel humiliated even before the excuses come out of your mouth, or who will show up at your doorstep with a burlap sack, a big rock, and a blindfold should you attempt to wiggle out of paying your debt. And make sure you bet something that's painful to lose but not too unrealistic. For example, you could bet someone a thousand dollars that you'll have the first chapter of your book written by a certain date. Make it a payable amount that you really don't want to pay, but that's barely within your reach. Then write the check out to him, include the payment date, and keep it over your desk to remind you what's in store if you don't get the job done. And if you really want to up the stakes, tell him that if you don't meet your deadline, instead of giving him the money, you'll donate the thousand dollars to a group or cause that makes your flesh crawl. Personally, I find this kind of horror works wonders for my self-discipline.

4. OWN IT AND WORK WITH IT

If you're the kind of person who blows everything off until the last minute, and you know this about yourself, why waste your time freaking out while you're not doing what you're supposed to be doing? Go to the damn beach, have a cocktail, and when the pressure's on, get down to business. There's nothing worse than time wasted pretending to work or stressing out while trying to have fun—no work gets done and no fun is had. It's the worst of both worlds. Figure out how much time you truly need to get the job done, and go do something else until the clock starts ticking.

5. LOVE YOURSELF

Right now, wherever you're at.

CHAPTER 19:

THE DRAMA OF OVERWHELM

I have lived a long life and had many troubles, most of which never happened.

—Mark Twain; American author, humorist

When I set out to write a new book, I find it very helpful to start with a separate index card for each chapter. I put the chapter title at the top of each card, write my notes in the space underneath, and then spread them all out on a table so I can see the whole thing at once. I just did this a few days ago and it was so exciting. Behold! My glorious new book! About two seconds later, however, I was seized by panic. *OMG that is a lot of chapters how the hell am I going to get it all done in time my deadline is speeding around the corner and I'm not even entirely sure what I'm putting in each section yet what was I thinking how come I didn't start this eight months ago is it too early for wine someone help me I am sinking . . .*

I closed my eyes and took a deep breath. *Just. Do. One. Chapter. At. A. Time.* So I pulled a random card off the table, opened my eyes, and it was, of course: The Drama of Overwhelm.

I'd like to remind you, and me, that the majority of the pain and suffering in our lives is caused by the unnecessary drama that we create. If we happen to find ourselves, for example, in a catatonic state of overwhelm, hugging our knees while rocking back and forth with our mouths hanging open, just like everything else in our lives, all it takes is a shift in perception to create a new reality.

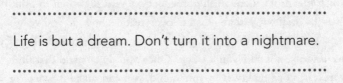

Life is but a dream. Don't turn it into a nightmare.

We are so unbelievably blessed to have all the things we have, all the opportunities and ideas and people and tasks and interests and experiences and responsibilities—choosing to freak out about it all, rather than enjoying the living of our lives, is like throwing pearls before swine. Such a waste of such a glorious gift.

In the interest of helping you get a more pleasant perspective on your massive to-do list, let's take the three most common complaints about overwhelm and pretty them up:

1. THERE'S NOT ENOUGH TIME

Thanks to the hard work of people with big brains, we now know that time is an illusion. While most people have no idea what the hell that means, there is another angle that's a lot easier to grasp; not having time is an illusion. For example:

I don't have time to find a real parking spot so I'll park in this loading

zone. Oh, look at that, I just spent three hours I don't have getting my car out
of the tow garage, another two getting lost on the way home, and forty-five min-
utes complaining about it to my wife.

I don't have time to clean my office. Oh, look at that, I just spent a half an
hour that I don't have looking for my phone that was buried beneath a pile of
crap. Oh, and look at that, my phone is dead, which means I'm about to waste
even more time I don't have looking for the damn charger which might be under
this pile of books over here please I hope . . .

When we're forced to do something, suddenly the time is there.
Which means it's there all the time, but we've just chosen to limit ourselves by believing that it isn't. Ever notice how if you've got six
months to do something, it'll take you six months to do it, but if you
have a week, it'll take you a week? Once you understand that time, like
the rest of your reality, is in your mind, you can make it work for you
instead of being its slave.

Here are some things you can do right now to start wrangling time
into submission:

SHOW SOME RESPECT

If you want more time in your life, show time some respect. If you're
constantly late, if you blow things off or if you're a flake, you're not
sending a message to The Universe—or others, or yourself—that you
value this precious time that you crave and are trying to create more
of for yourself.

You can create anything you desire, but you have to
truly want it.

If you act like time isn't important, that it's fully worth wasting and disrespecting, you're not in alignment with what you say you want so you're gonna have a hard time getting it. I mean, think of time as a person. Would you expect time to keep showing up for you if you constantly treated it like it was just some dumb thing that didn't matter? I should think not.

If you're always late, start being early. If you constantly cancel or flake or forget your dates with people, get it together. Write down your appointments and keep them. Set your alarm on your cell phone to remind you to get ready. Early. Write things on the back of your hands. Keep your word if you say you're going to do something. It's not rocket science—if you want to have a good relationship with time, have a good relationship with time. Not only will this help you create more time in your own life, but you'll stop being one of those rude people who constantly wastes everyone else's.

KEEP YOUR FRIENDS CLOSE AND YOUR ENEMIES CLOSER

What do you find yourself doing instead of doing what you're supposed to be doing? Screwing around on Facebook? Answering e-mails? Eating even though you're not hungry? Once you know what your favorite distractions are, you can build up a good defense against them. Turn off the Internet and phone while you're working. Make the kitchen off-limits until you're done if you constantly find yourself standing in front of the open refrigerator door in a stupor. We get into such bad habits that half the time we don't even realize what we're doing. Once you become aware of what your weak spots are, you can start to protect yourself against them.

CHUNK IT DOWN

There's nothing more deflating than looking at some giant task and wondering how you'll ever get it all done. So don't try and eat the whole elephant at once, break it down into bite-sized bits. For example, instead of walking around your entire house, from one catastrophically messy room to the next, wondering how you're ever going to clean the whole gigantic thing (and trying to figure out how you can justify not doing it instead of trying to figure out how you're going to do it) break it down and just focus on one room at a time. Our brains can only handle so much information at once without exploding, so by looking at each task separately, the larger task suddenly becomes more manageable.

Brains love chunks.

Chunking it down works great for time too. For example, if you're working on designing a new website, instead of setting aside the entire day to work, decide that you'll work in hour-long chunks. During this time you are unauthorized to get up to use the bathroom, get something to eat, check your texts, go online, etc. Once your sixty minutes is up, you can take a break and do whatever you want until your next sixty-minute chunk. We can do anything for sixty minutes. Our brains go into overwhelm when we try to do it all in one big block of time.

2. THERE'S TOO MUCH TO DO

Ever notice that whenever you ask someone how they're doing, about 99 percent of the time they say something like "Good. Really busy, but good." "Busy" has become the new "Fine, thanks." I mean, where's the fun in that? What kind of message does that send out to the world and ourselves? No wonder we all feel like we're living pinned beneath a giant, cement slab of a to-do list. So, yes, the first task is to:

WATCH YOUR MOUTH

Stop talking about how busy you are. Focus on what you enjoy about what you do and the spaces in between the doing instead of feeling weighed down by it all. Decide that you live an awesome, relaxed life full of interesting projects that you love doing and communicate that to the world and yourself. And then go out and merrily do it.

GET SOME HELP

If you're feeling totally confused and disorganized and don't know where to start or what to do next, get some outside perspective. A lot of times we're so tangled up in our own lives that we can't see something that's totally obvious to someone else. Ever spend some quality time searching for your glasses when they're sitting right on your head? It's sort of like that. You could spend hours or days or months (or forever) trying to figure out how to re-do your website or plotting out an exercise regimen or figuring out how to organize your office, when someone who isn't as buried alive by all the moving parts as you are can nail it right away. Get a new pair of eyeballs on the situation.

And get someone who knows what they're doing please. Don't get money advice from someone who's as broke as you are or dating advice from the terminally single or decide that someone's main qualification for helping you is that they'll do it for free or trade. Working with a pro will save you time and money in the long run because you won't have to spend time undoing, or doing over, whatever your wimpy first attempt was.

Hire a business coach, ask a friend who is totally together and successful to sit with you, hire a clutter consultant, and if none of this makes sense for your particular situation, read on:

GET INTO REALITY

Sometimes we take on more than we can chew because we think we have to do it all. Or that the world will fall apart if we don't do everything. Or that we are bad, unlovable people if we don't do the eight million things we're trying to do. So get very real with yourself here— why are you doing all the things you're doing? Is it absolutely necessary that you do it all? Do you need to do it all at the same time? Can some of it wait? Be handed off to someone else? Dropped altogether? And if you must do it all, what would make it more enjoyable?

Just like chunking down your time, chunking down your tasks takes you out of freak-out and puts things into manageable, bite-sized pieces. Here's how to break it down:

Make your to-do list. Look at it.

> What needs to happen right now?
>
> What can wait?
>
> Put these on two separate lists. Hide the Wait list.
>
> What are the big important tasks on the Now list?
>
> What are the little piddly ones?

Give the piddly ones to someone else or save them for off hours and spend the day doing the most important tasks. It's called prioritizing people!

The shorter the list you're working with, the better you'll feel.

And remember: *You're never gonna get it all done.* So stop stressing about it.

. . . .

Do what you can do in joy, instead of trying to do it all in misery.

. . . .

DELEGATE OR DIE

One of the best ways to lighten your load is to stop being a control freak and/or a tightwad and hire someone to help you. Or delegate to those around you (see below).

You absolutely cannot grow a business, get promoted or be a cool parent, and you absolutely will go gray before your time, if you try and do every single little thing by yourself.

Figure out which tasks you hate doing or have always been bad at or just don't have time to do and find someone else to do them. I realize the reason you may not have done this yet is because you can't afford to hire someone, or because you think you're the best at it, or because you're a control freak, but, like many other excuses, the answer is often there, you're just not looking at it properly. If you absolutely had to get some help, if it was a matter of life or death, what would you do? You could get an intern from your local college. You could get a friend or family member to help you out. You could hire someone for just thirty minutes a week and increase as you go. You could sell something to bring in the money to pay someone. Or borrow it. Or push yourself to make it. You could hand it over to human resources and make it their problem. You could ask your husband to empty the dishwasher and get your teenager to clean out the garage so you'd have more time. Help is all around us, sometimes receiving it is simply a matter of looking at it differently, or not giving up so easily.

Deciding that you can't have something you need or want instantly cuts you off from the flow of manifesting it, as well as distances you from the part that lit you up about it in the first place. Once you think "I can't," The Universe is like, "Alrighty then, no assistance needed here, see you later." Even if you have no idea where it's going to come from, stay open to the possibility of support presenting itself and you may be surprised by what you can create and how much help you can get. Decide you must have it, trust that it's available to you, do everything you can to figure out a way to make it happen and trust that *how* it's going to happen will be revealed.

REMEMBER THAT YOU ARE #1

Put your priorities first—don't check e-mails or voice messages or Facebook until you've gotten into your day and accomplished some of the tasks you want to do. Don't answer the phone or texts while you're busy. Other people's needs can occupy several lifetimes' worth of our attention, and if you let them, they will.

3. I'M EXHAUSTED

The belief that taking time off will cause your entire life to collapse is not only unhealthy, but it's arrogant (the world will go on if you stop working, you see). If you don't take time off, your body will eventually put its foot down and make you sick. Bodies do it all the time. Stress is a leading cause of cancer, heart attacks, liver failure, stupid accidents, grouchiness, and suddenly not being able to breathe.

Aside from the sickness factor, making time to do the things that inspire you should also be a priority because, um, what's the point of living life without them? Where's the fun in waking up at eighty-five and realizing you "couldn't find the time" to enjoy yourself? What were you doing that was more important instead? This is not a luxury reserved for people who are richer, smarter, or less bogged down than you are. It's a luxury reserved for people who take the time to figure it out and choose to design a more fun-filled life.

Use the tools in this chapter to make the time to get the rest you need and have the fun you want so you can enjoy your precious life while you're still in possession of it.

4. LOVE YOURSELF

You're doing an awesome job.

CHAPTER 20:

FEAR IS FOR SUCKERS

We tiptoe through life hoping to safely make it to death.

—Unknown

When I lived in New Mexico, a friend of mine took me to this cave she'd heard about up in the Jemez Mountains. "It's more like a big hole in the ground, actually," she said, "but I hear it's pretty cool." She didn't do a great job of selling it, especially when she got to the part about how we'd have to crawl around on all fours the whole time, but I wasn't really listening to her anyway. Caves don't interest me, no matter what size they are; I was only going for the road trip and the hike through the mountains and this great burger place that I discovered the last time I was up there. The cave was just a necessary part of the trip, like stopping for gas.

After a glorious drive beneath the endless New Mexico sky and a beautiful hike on a red dirt path through a piñon pine forest, we got to The Cave. It was just as she'd described: a little hole at the base of a small hill just big enough to crawl through. My friend tossed me a pair of knee pads and a flashlight and headed in. I followed her on my hands and knees, holding my flashlight with my teeth, and by the time we were about ten minutes in, I felt like the entrance, and my chances of ever seeing another burger again, had vanished. If anything came at us from inside the cave, like, say, a monster, or if there was a flash flood or an earthquake or a rattlesnake or a mosquito, we were totally screwed. The craggy white rock tunnel surrounding us had closed in so tightly that when my friend finally stopped crawling and leaned against the wall to sit, she had to do so with her head bent so far forward it looked like she was about to start chewing on her neck. What the hell was I doing there again?

"Okay, now for the cool part—you ready?" she asked. "Turn off your light." She clicked off her flashlight after motioning for me to do the same. The instant my light went out, I experienced the absolute darkest darkness of beyond pitch-black holy fucking shit deepest darkest blackness ever. I felt the tickling of hysteria begin to worm its way up the back of my neck, and for the first time in my life, I completely understood fear.

Because fear was the only thing I could see in that hole. It sat there, omnipresent, gigantic, all consuming, staring me straight in the face asking, "So, you gonna let me swallow you up or what?"

I realized that with absolutely zero effort, I could unravel into a claustrophobic freak-out of such scratching, biting, high-pitched crazy-lady screaming colossal-ness, that it would leave both me and my friend staring at a wall, playing with our lips for weeks after they dragged our limp and bloodied bodies out of that cave.

Or . . . not.

The choice was mine.

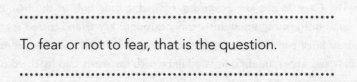

To fear or not to fear, that is the question.

I'm pleased to report that I decided to forego the fear frenzy in favor of calmly crawling back out of the cave to the land of sunshine, open spaces, and walking on two legs. I emerged with not only an alarming amount of sand in my ears and severe lockjaw from cracking the flashlight with my teeth, but with a new and profound understanding of the *choice* aspect of fear.

It's so simple; fear will always be there, poised and ready to wreak havoc, but we can choose whether we're going to engage with it or turn on the lights, drown it out and crawl past it. I also realized that drowning it out is actually pretty easy, we've just been conditioned to believe otherwise.

We've made being in fear a habit.

We're pumped full of it as children, like sugar, then as we grow we continue to take in the bad news on TV and the horror in the papers and the violence in books and films and video games and all this junk that fills us to the brim with fear about our world. We're taught to play it safe and not take risks, and to caution everyone around us to follow suit.

And it's become such an accepted part of our social conditioning that we don't even realize we're doing it.

For example, what would your immediate response be to someone you really loved and deeply cared about if they said, whilst sputtering with excitement, any of the following things to you:

I'm taking out a gigantic loan to build my dream business.

I'm going to travel around the world. For a year. By myself.

I'm quitting my secure, full-time job to become an actor.

I met the most incredible person last week and I'm totally in love. And we're getting married.

I'm going skydiving.

For the most part, when we watch someone take a leap of faith, our first reaction is to scream, "Look out!" We've not only made a habit out of smearing our fear and worry and doubt all over each other, but we pat ourselves on the backs for it because we believe that it shows how much we care.

THAT's something worth being scared of, if you ask me.

There's something called the Crab Effect. If you put a bunch of crabs in a bowl and if, while they're in there crawling all over each other, one of them tries to climb out, the rest of them will try to pull him back down instead of helping to push him out. No wonder they're called crabs.

Imagine how different our world would be if *we* were less crab-like. If we were not only taught to *really truly* believe in miracles, yes, I realize how dorky that sounds, but were rewarded and supported, instead of cautioned and screamed at, for taking huge leaps into the unknown. We give a lot of lip service to the idea that anything is possible, and we all grow up with posters of kittens and baby seals on our walls that say *follow your dreams* on them, but should you actually *do* something radical, all the flashing lights and sirens go off. Know what I'm sayin'?

Fear lives in the future. The feeling of being afraid is real, but the fear itself is all made up *because it hasn't even happened yet*—death, going bankrupt, breaking a leg, forgetting our lines, getting yelled at for being late, getting rejected, etc. Most of the time we have no guarantee that what we fear is going to even happen and that if it does, that it's going to be scary! Take death for example. For all we know we leave our bodies and melt into a state of pure love and light and sparkly things and unicorns and bunnies eternal orgasmic giddiness. We can be as sure of that as we can about anything else in the future, so why create all the drama?

All it takes to turn the fear factor around is learning to be comfortable in, instead of terrified of, the unknown. And this is done through faith.

It basically comes down to how you choose to go through life:

··

Is your fear greater than your faith in the unknown (and yourself)?

Or is your faith in the unknown (and yourself) greater than your fear?

··

While you're making your choice, here's a mouthful from good old Helen Keller:

Life is either a daring adventure, or nothing. To keep our faces toward change and behave like free spirits in the presence of fate is strength undefeatable.

There's that incredible moment when you decide, "screw it, I'm going for it," and suddenly the thrill overtakes the fear. And then you're flying on the magic carpet—you're signing on the dotted line to buy the house, confronting your father, sliding the ring onto the finger, stepping onto the stage in front of thousands. I mean, talk about feeling alive!

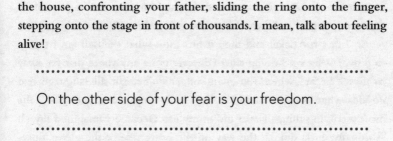

On the other side of your fear is your freedom.

Here are some helpful ways to navigate your way through the jungle of fear:

1. VIEW FEAR FROM YOUR REAR VIEW MIRROR

Think about some radical thing you did in the past that literally gave you the shakes it was so big and scary. And now look back on it—how terrifying is it now? Can you conjure up any scary feelings about it? Even a weensy twinge of fear? Keep this in mind as you face each new challenge: No matter how intimidating your next great leap forward seems at the moment, it will be a pipsqueak when you look back on it someday. So why wait? Why not look at it through pipsqueak colored glasses right now? Envision your challenges from the future, look back on them from a place of victory, and they will lose much of their power to paralyze you.

I always use my first trip to India as an example when I'm being a weenie about doing something that scares me. It was one of my very first international solo trips, and even though my experience with anything Indian up to that point pretty much consisted of a couple Ravi Shankar CDs and some chicken tikka masala, I thought it would be such a cool place to see. I wanted to go somewhere totally new and experience a reality that was as different from my own as possible. I thought going to India would be like going through the looking glass.

So I buy my ticket and then it hits me—what the hell am I trying to prove? Why am I doing this? I'd never gone anywhere that far away by myself before, where I knew no one, didn't speak the language, had no idea what to expect, and I swear I built it up to become one of the most terrifying things I ever did in my life. Because I imagined myself as this tiny little dot, all the way on the other side of the globe, floating around in space where I was utterly anonymous, a ghost, a stranger, where I could disappear without a trace and nobody I loved would have any idea what happened to me. Poof!

It got so bad that I started fantasizing about seriously injuring myself or that my best friend would die so I wouldn't have to go (for some reason, just canceling my ticket never entered my mind). As luck would have it, however, nobody died, and I found myself being driven to the airport like I was going to my own funeral. The moment I stepped into the international terminal at the airport, however, I was swept up in a sea of colors and people from all over the world and movement and languages and my terror was instantly bulldozed by excitement. I'm going to freakin' India!

When I got on the plane, I sat next to this gorgeous Indian woman wearing a pink sari and huge gold earrings who turned to me, smiled, and offered me an M&M and that's when it really sank in; *You're not alone you ding dong. You are surrounded by people. And one of the most basic common human needs is connection.* I then proceeded to spend two months traveling around a country that is now by far one of my favorite places on this planet and that sparked in me a love for travel that has completely changed my life.

This, and other examples from my own life, keep proving to me over and over that:

Our greatest fears are the greatest waste of time.

Face your fears with the truth, that they are all in your mind, and they will lose their power over you.

2. FLIP THE FEAR

When you find yourself letting fear push you around, look at it from a different perspective. Start by breaking it down, finding what it is that you're really afraid of and then flipping it around to make it work for you, not against you. Show it who's boss. Feed your fear a suck-it sandwich.

For example:

I want to write a book but can't get myself to sit down and do it. Why not? *I'm scared that if I do it will be terrible.* What happens if it's terrible? *If it's terrible I'll look stupid.* Then what? *People will make fun of me.* Then what? *I'll feel ashamed.* Okay, so you're not writing your book in order to protect yourself from feeling stupid and ashamed.

Now flip it: How stupid and ashamed will you feel if you don't write your book? *Very. I know it's a brilliant idea. And it's a big dream of mine.* So will your strategy of not writing it in order to protect yourself from feeling stupid and ashamed protect you from feeling stupid and ashamed? *No.* And since you're risking feeling stupid and ashamed either way, which version is worse—trying to write it and having it be terrible or never going for it and living an unlived life of mediocrity, wimpiness, and shame? *Living an unlived life of mediocrity, wimpiness, and shame.*

Break it down so you can really look at, and defuse, what it is about a situation that's scaring you. Fear is all about how you choose to look at things, so by changing your perspective on it you can let the fear of NOT doing the thing you're scared of fuel your quest to greatness.

3. BE IN THE MOMENT

Is anything scary happening to you right now at this very moment? Right now, where you're sitting, is anything bad actually happening or is it just the thoughts in your head that are freaking you out? You deplete the much-needed energy you need to kick ass by freaking out before something even happens. Instead, stay in the moment and connect to your higher self. If you're about to walk into the courtroom or jump out of a plane or ask for a raise, breathe into the moment and stay connected to Source Energy. Keep your frequency high and your belief in miracles strong instead of falling prey to the fears in your mind, and you'll find that not only are you much better equipped to deal with whatever situation it is that you're headed for, but that, nine times out of ten, it's much scarier in your mind than it is in reality.

4. CUT OFF THE STREAM OF CRAP

Be more conscious of the information you absorb. What blogs do you read? What shows do you watch? What books do you read? What stories do you read in the paper? What movies do you go to? Whose opinion do you ask? What do you focus on in your day-to-day life? This isn't about being in denial or out of touch with what's going on in the world, it's about how much of this information you really need. Are you staring at a car accident or are you gathering information that will allow you to contribute to positive change?

Wallowing in the pain and suffering isn't going to help anyone, yourself included, any more than starving yourself will help the hungry. If you want to help the world and yourself, keep your frequency high and do your work from a place of power and joy.

5. DON'T THINK OF ANYTHING UPSETTING IN BED AT NIGHT

Our minds turn into gigantic magnifying glasses that make all our fears 100 percent bigger when we're lying there as a captive audience at 3 a.m., in bed, with nothing to distract us. Unless you're going to get out of bed right then and there and take some sort of action, don't waste your precious time thinking about your problems. Every time you do this, it's never as bad the next morning when you get up. You know this and yet . . . Use your meditative powers to move troubling thoughts out of your mind; focus on relaxing every single muscle in your body one by one, slowly and intentionally, so that it takes up all the room in your brain that you were using to freak out with. Breathe deeply and think about all the incredible things in your life, listen to a guided meditation, do whatever you can to get a good night's sleep and deal with whatever it is in the morning. Because the only thing worse than staying up all night freaking out about something is then being too exhausted the next day to deal with it either.

6. LOVE YOURSELF

And you will be invincible.

CHAPTER 21:

MILLIONS OF MIRRORS

No one can make you feel inferior without your consent.
—Eleanor Roosevelt; activist, feminist, superhero,
longest-serving First Lady of the United States evah

One of the most staggering things about other people is that they provide us with valuable, and often alarmingly intimate, information about who they are as soon as we meet them. If we pay attention, we can pick up on the major clues they're sending out through their body language, their appearance, their lifestyle, their actions, their interests, their words, how they treat their dogs, the waitress, themselves, etc. Some people let it all hang out for everyone to see right away, others let it seep out in little spurts: "I love water skiing," "I admire how confident you are about your weight problem," "I just got out of prison," etc. With the exception of the sociopath or the skilled pathological liar, the majority of humanity gives us plenty to chew on right out of the gate.

All of this information then goes through the filter of who *we* are, and depending on our perceptions and judgments and hang ups and number of years spent in therapy, we decide if the person is someone we want to get to know better or not.

We're all attracted to, as well as turned off by, various things about other people. And the things that stand out the most to us are the things that remind us the most of ourselves. This is because other people are like mirrors for us: If somebody bugs you, you're projecting onto them something that you don't like about yourself, and if you think they're awesome, they're reflecting back something that you see in yourself that you like (even if it's not developed in you yet). I know this sounds like I'm making a massive generalization, but just stay with me here.

Your reality is created by what you focus on and how you choose to interpret it. This goes for everything, including the things you focus on about the people in your world. For example, depending on who you are, you could react in myriad ways to your new boyfriend or girlfriend constantly referring to you as "The Giant Dumbass." You could A) See this as a red flag and think they're a bully B) See this as a red flag and think they're nervous or insecure and have terrible manners C) See this as a green light because "they are in so much pain that they need to abuse other people. They really need someone as understanding as I am" D) See this as a green light because you believe that you are, in fact, a giant dumbass or E.) Think it's hilarious because it doesn't resonate with you.

....

The people you surround yourself with are excellent mirrors for who you are and how much, or how little, you love yourself.

....

We attract people into our lives for a reason, just as they attract us into theirs. We all help each other grow and figure out our issues, *if* we seize the opportunity to learn from, instead of just react to (by getting defensive or justifying our actions or whining about), the highly irritating things other people do. It's our annoying friends or family members or clients or neighbors or lady on the train with the voice like a bullhorn who help us grow and see who we truly are even more than our beloved BFFs do (unless they're being momentarily annoying, and then we can thank them, too). Don't miss the glorious opportunity to learn that's being handed to you by the person whose mouth you'd really love to stick your fist in.

The things that bother us about other people bother us because they remind us of something that we don't like about ourselves. Or their behavior triggers a fear or insecurity that we have, but may not realize we have. For the longest time, one of my big stories was that being feminine was weak and annoying. Somewhere along the way I decided that it wasn't cool or powerful to act like (or be) a girl, and my femininity became a part of me that I was ashamed of. Hence, I was much less threatened by women who came at me with a power drill than women who came at me with an eyebrow pencil, which is why it's pretty hilarious to me still that one of my best friends is as girly as they get. I met her when we were working together in New York City and was instantly drawn to her because she's hilariously brilliant and sweet and did a flawless impression of one of our coworkers walking down the hall with his ass sticking out that always left me doubled over, clinging to furniture. Unlike me, however, she's a lover of girls' nights out and mani-pedi dates, an eager ogler of engagement rings when summoned by the fluttering hand of a soon-to-be bride, and a pro at the girly-girl gang greeting: Arms raised high in the air, head back, eyes squeezed shut, high-pitched Oh-my-Gods for all to hear. For this, we call her Pink.

A decade later, I'm living in Los Angeles and Pink is living outside

New York City— married with a bunch of kids, natch. When she decides to take her first solo vacation since becoming a mom, and heads to San Diego to see her best friend from college, she calls and begs me to drive down to see her. I agree, somewhat begrudgingly. It wasn't the two-hour drive that bothered me, but the best friend from college, who I'd never met but was sure was pinker than Pink. I imagined a full-on sorority scene, complete with painting our toenails while having a Meg Ryan movie fest and talking about how fat we'd gotten. But I love Pink, so off I went.

Meanwhile, down in San Diego, Pink's best friend from college is less than thrilled at the prospect of Pink's best gal pal from her New York City days driving down from L.A. Her eyes were also rolling at the potential estrogen bomb, so imagine our delight when we discovered that we were both equally as macho. Once we realized that the playing field wasn't as overwhelmingly pink as we feared it would be, however, we got the biggest surprise of all: our inner, neglected girls felt safe to come out hiding. All three of us lost our voices that weekend, cackling and screaming, "Oh my God," for all to hear. I wouldn't be surprised if a toenail or two even got painted. Don't remember. Was too drunk on wine spritzers.

I'm still not the most enthused member of a bridal shower, and I'm not saying that you have to come around and like everything in this world that bothers you, but I am saying that if you *actively* don't like something, it's because it resonates with you on some level, it has meaning to you.

When you find yourself dealing with someone who irritates you (and you find yourself getting gossipy, fingerpointy, judgy, complainey), rising up and confronting the situation can do a hell of a lot more than just making your life more pleasant in the long run; it can help you heal and grow and get out of victim mode. Because it forces you to deal with the gnarlier aspects of yourself, the parts that make you not so proud. None of us care to admit that we're dishonest, conceited, insecure, unethical, mean, bossy, stupid, lazy, etc., but that's what attracted you to the people you notice it in, and them to you, in the first place. And admitting it is the first step in letting it go—wheeee!

If people are annoying in a way that has nothing to do with us, we either don't notice it or we don't get that hung up on it. For example, say there's someone in your life who you find to be an insufferable know-it-all. Every time you open your mouth to talk about something you did, she says she's already done it. Anything you know, she already knows. And knows much more about. And she has to make sure you, and everyone within a ten mile radius, knows how much more she knows about it. While you find yourself entertaining fantasies about putting her head through the wall every time you're around her, someone else might be hanging on her every word, unable to get enough of her fascinating and brilliant conversation.

The reason she makes you crazy is because you most likely are a know-it-all yourself, or you worry that you are one, or you have insecurities about people thinking that you know nothing.

Our reality is a mirror of our thoughts, the people in our reality included.

Same thing goes with what people throw at us. Would you be offended if someone kept making fun of how short you were if you were six feet tall? It most likely wouldn't even register, or if it did, you'd just think they were kind of strange. But if they teased you about being bossy, and deep down you feared you were, it would definitely get your attention. (It would also mean they have energy around their own bossiness if they're recognizing it in you, but that's not your problem.)

What you focus on you create more of in your life. If you're consciously or subconsciously focused on certain beliefs about who you are, or who you want to be or who you do not want to be, you will attract people who mirror those traits right back at you.

This is why, when you're dealing with a backstabbing "friend" or some sort of toxic person that you need to stand up to or kick out of your life, you get caught in this self-inflicted trap of not wanting to hurt the other person or latching on to their finer qualities or fearing the worst if you don't put up with their crap. I don't care how long you've been friends with someone or how sorry you feel for them or how they really helped you those eight million times or how hilarious, successful, hot, inspiring, desperate, scary, connected, brilliant, or helpless they are, because the reason you're having trouble standing up to them isn't about any of that.

What's really going on is you're being faced with rewiring your limited beliefs about *yourself.* And you're using these excuses for these other people to avoid facing your own issues—your own issues around sticking up for yourself.

....

At the end of the day, it's not about them, it's about you believing you're worthy of being loved and seen for who you really are.

....

When we agree to let ourselves down in favor of supporting the bad behavior of others, it often stems from the same impulse: *We're unwilling to make other people more uncomfortable than they just made us.* Not terribly sturdy in the old self-love department, is it? By making them uncomfortable I mean *declining to participate in their drama,* by the way, not by being equally abusive back. This isn't about getting an eye for an eye and sinking to a lower level, it's about standing up for your highest self no matter if the person you're dealing with should choose to have the experience of:

- Feeling disappointed
- Feeling hurt
- Feeling inconvenienced
- Seeing you as a crazy person

....

It's about respecting yourself, instead of catering to your insecure need to be liked.

....

This is incredibly powerful, because *when you love yourself enough to stand in your truth no matter what the cost, everyone benefits.* You start attracting the kinds of things, people, and opportunities, that are in alignment with who you truly are, which is way more fun than hanging out with a bunch of irritating energy suckers. And by declining to participate in other people's drama, (i.e. refusing to rip people to shreds, to complain about how unfair the world is, etc.) you not only raise your own frequency, but you offer the drama queens the chance to rise up too, instead of everyone continuing to play a low, lame game.

....

Never apologize for who you are. It lets the whole world down.

....

We all know someone who does not take shit from anyone. Ever. We look upon these types of people with wide-eyed reverence, and would never dream of being stupid enough to present them with any of our BS or try to make them wrong. Why? Because we respect them and, um, are usually kind of terrified of them (in a healthy way). And why do we respect them? *Because they respect themselves.*

So how can you get rid of your lame-o projections and judgments and grace the world with your highest, most unapologetic self?

1. OWN YOUR UGLY

Start noticing the things that drive you nuts about other people, and, instead of complaining or judging or getting defensive about them, use them as a mirror. *Especially if you find yourself getting really worked up.* Get mighty real with yourself—is this quality something you have yourself? Or is there a certain aspect to it that you're loath to admit is just like you? Or does it remind you of something you're actively trying to suppress? Or avoid? Or that you're actively doing just the opposite of? Or that you're threatened by? Become fascinated by, instead of furious about, the irritants surrounding you and get yer learnin' on.

2. QUESTION YOUR UGLY

Once you discover what part of yourself you're projecting onto the person who is presently bugging the living crap out of you, you can start letting it go. Begin by asking yourself some very simple questions and defusing the limiting and false stories you've been lugging around for ages.

For example, if you're all pissed off that your friend who's always late is late again, it's pushing your buttons because you're holding on to some sort of "truth" about the way people should be with time. Flip it around and ask yourself things like, "In what ways am I always late or inconsiderate or unreliable?" Or maybe it's "In what ways am I'm too rigid or controlling?"

Once you have your answer, ask yourself:

WHO DO I NEED TO BE FOR THIS SITUATION NOT TO BOTHER ME?

Using the above scenario, let's say you discover that you're a lot more rigid than you care to admit. This is very valuable information because you now know that in order to be happier, you need to loosen your bone, Wilma. Stop insisting that people do things exactly the way you do them (especially the people in your life who have proven they most definitely won't), notice where you're being ridiculously demanding simply because it's become your habit, and not because it's really necessary, and constantly ask yourself "can I let this one go?" By becoming aware of what we do, we can investigate why we do it and then choose to keep it or drop it, instead of blindly reacting through habit.

WHAT AM I GETTING OUT OF BEING THIS WAY?

As discussed in Chapter 17: It's So Easy Once You Figure Out It Isn't Hard, we don't do anything unless we're getting something out of it, even if what we're getting are false benefits. Using this scenario, some of the positive benefits of being rigid are that you're always on time, you get shit done, etc. But there are also some negative advantages to being rigid too; you intimidate people into getting your way, you get to be right whenever someone messes up (which they'll do often if you've really honed the rigid thing well), you get to be in control, etc.

Once you bust yourself on the false reward you're getting from holding on to this behavior, you can see it for what it is—something that's not always in alignment with who you truly are and aspire to be—and release it when it's not working.

HOW WOULD I FEEL IF I WASN'T THIS WAY?

One of the best ways to release the aforementioned lousy behavior is by asking yourself how you'd feel if this wasn't true for you anymore. "How would I feel if I took the pole out of my ass about everyone doing everything exactly how I say to do it, all the time, in every circumstance?" Ask the question and then imagine yourself as this person who has let it go. How does your body feel? What do you use the brain space for that used to be taken up with poisonous thoughts about the inconsiderate pinheads you're surrounded by who are not following your instructions? Feel into the reality of what it would be to let this go, breathe into it, visualize it, fall in love with not having it anymore, and then kick it to the curb.

3. DON'T BE AN ENABLER

In the fuzzier cases where you're not sure what to do, but you really do want to help someone, recognize the difference between helping and enabling. When you reach out a helping hand, do you feel like they're pulling you down or that you're lifting them up toward their potential? Are they grateful or entitled? Do they use your help to actively move themselves in a positive direction or do they constantly need more-more-more? Just this one last time. For the fiftieth time.

Pay attention and trust how you feel. If you're truly helping them and they're rising to the occasion, it will raise everyone's frequencies and you'll feel good. If you're enabling them, you'll feel heavy, depressed, and eventually resentful. While it's no fun to kick someone to the curb when they're at their lowest low, if you constantly bail them out, they'll never wake up and save themselves. Why should they? They've got you to fund their pity party. Tough love is still love.

4. GIVE PAINFUL PEOPLE THE HEAVE-HO

Sometimes, no matter how much work you do on yourself and how forgiving you are and how skilled you get at letting it go, there's just no way around it: Some people are just too committed to their own dysfunction. They're painful to be around. You'd rather cover yourself with the fleas of a thousand camels than go out for a cup of coffee with them.

This is all about learning and loving and growing into the highest version of yourself, not seeing just how much torture you can endure. So along with understanding how to grow from the not-so-savory behavior of those around you, it's also important to understand how to get the hell away from them if they're chronically self-obsessed or violent or blaming or negative or controlling or jealous or high drama or manipulative or victimized or whiney or pessimistic or mean to animals. Here's how:

FIRST, FEED YOUR HEAD

As discussed, lot of times the people we need to kick to the curb happen to be those we love, or at least like a lot, for their decent qualities. Hence ye olde guilt can really get in our way when trying to do the right thing. So stay strong. See it as being nice to yourself instead of being mean to them. Remembering that you are rising up to be the highest version of yourself instead of shrinking down to their level can give you the strength you need to shake them off your leg.

NEXT, HIT EJECT

Another important thing to remember when yanking the weeds out of your garden is not to get involved in their drama. Cut the cord as quickly and simply as possible, with little to no discussion. If they're so oblivious to your feelings that you need to toss them out of your life, chances are very good they won't see this coming, so the discussion on why you need to end it could go on for the rest of your lives if you let it. Suddenly get really busy, fade them out, wean them off you with zero explanation. The louder they scream, the busier you suddenly get.

If having a conversation is unavoidable, remember: You've already decided that you want out, so don't get sucked into working through your decision, or their problems, with them. Simply say that the relationship isn't working for you, that you don't like how it makes you feel, that you have to end it, and that it's not open for discussion. Make it all about you, give them nothing to work with or argue on their behalf.

5. LOVE YOURSELF

Fiercely, loyally, unapologetically.

CHAPTER 22:

THE SWEET LIFE

It's great to be here. It's great to be anywhere.
—**Keith Richards; Rock God, connoisseur of life**

I've got a cat who's twenty-two years old.

I've also got a dad who's eighty-seven.

The cat and my dad share the same superhero power: They both have the ability to make me pay lots of attention to them and be nicer to them than I am to anyone else. Anyone else not staring down the barrel of their impending mortality, that is.

I first realized that my cat was old and might die soon about a year ago when, overnight, all his body fat plunged to his belly region, causing him to swing it around like an udder and leaving him with a spine that's still in shock, jutting out all spindly and jagged, wondering where everybody went. This is when the teary farewells started every time I'd leave the house and the fancy wet food began appearing in his bowl.

In Dad's case, the phone calls and flights back east have escalated dramatically, and I now laugh hysterically at all his jokes, no doubt making him worry more about my well being than I do about his.

I'm thrilled to report that even though in the calendar's opinion, they're real old, they're both still kicking butt. Dad plays tennis once a week and still knows who I am, and my cat still runs when he hears the can opener.

They are also excellent reminders: When it comes to the creatures you love and the things you love and the life you love, what on earth could possibly be more important than soaking them up right now while you still have the opportunity?

If it's something you want to do, don't wait until you're less busy or richer or "ready" or twenty pounds lighter. Start right now. You'll never be this young again.

If it's the people you love, visit them as often as possible. Act as if every time you see them will be the last. If they bug you sometimes, love them anyway. If you've got differences, get over them. Don't get so tangled up in the stupid little stuff that you miss out on enjoying the people who have part-ownership of your heart.

If you're not where you want to be in life, keep going. Treat yourself like you're the closest friend you've got. Celebrate the magnificent creature that you are. Don't let anyone mess with you and your dreams, least of all yourself.

Your life is happening right now. Do not snooze and lose.

LOVE YOURSELF

While you've still got the chance.

PART 5:
HOW TO KICK
SOME ASS

CHAPTER 23:

THE ALMIGHTY DECISION

Until one is committed, there is hesitancy, the chance to draw back, always ineffectiveness. The moment one definitely commits one-self, then providence moves too.

—W.H. Murray; explorer, mountain climber, committer

The story goes that when Henry Ford first came up with the idea for his V-8 motor, he wanted the engine to have all eight cylinders cast in one block. I have no idea what that means, but apparently it was a tall order because his team of engineers was like, "Bitch, you crazy!" He told them to do it anyway, and off they grumbled to toil away at it, only to come back and inform him that it was impossible.

Upon hearing this news, Ford told them to keep at it, no matter how long it took. He was all, "I don't want to see your faces until you bring me what I want," and they were all, "We just proved it can't be done," and he was all, "It can be done and it will be done," and they were all, "Can not," and he was all, "Can so," and they were all, "No way," and he was all, "Way," so off they went again, this time for a whole year, and . . . nothing.

So they go back to Ford and there's lots of tears and finger-pointing and hair pulling and Ford sends them off *again*, and tells them it will be done *again* and then, in the lab, somewhere between folding origami swans out of their notes and making fart noises every time someone mentions the word "Ford," his engineers do the impossible. They discover how to make his eight-cylinder engine block.

This is what it means to make a decision *for reals.*

When you make a no-nonsense decision, you sign up fully and keep moving toward your goal, regardless of what's flung in your path. And stuff will most definitely get flung, which is why making the decision is so crucial—this shit is not for sissies. The moment it gets hard or expensive or puts you at risk of looking like a moron, if you haven't made the decision, you'll quit. If it wasn't uncomfortable, everyone would be out there all in love with their fabulous lives.

• •

So often, we pretend we've made a decision, when what we've really done is signed up to try until it gets too uncomfortable.

• •

Henry Ford didn't even make it past the sixth grade and there he was, bossing around a bunch of the world's biggest engineering smarty-pants, setting himself up to look like a total idiot by spending large amounts of money and time on the proven impossible.

Ford was determined. And he trusted his gut and his vision more than the small thinking of others. He'd made the decision that he would have his engine the way he would have it and nothing was going to stop him.

This is why the decision is so important. If you had an idea and had to go up against a roomful of people who "knew better" than you did, and demand they do what you say in spite of all the proof they had against you, would you stick to your guns? Or if you needed tens of thousands of dollars to start your new business, and the only person you could think of to ask was your scary, rich uncle who never remembered who you were even though you saw him every Christmas, would you ask him for it? Or if you were sick of feeling fat and unsexy and out of shape and the only time you could make it to the gym was at 5 a.m. on freezing winter mornings when you were all snuggly in bed, would you go? If you made the *decision* that you were going to reach your goals, you would do whatever it took. If you merely wanted to, but hadn't made the firm decision to, you'd roll over and begin convincing yourself that your life is fine just the way it is.

This is where being connected to your desire and Source Energy, and having an unshakable belief in the not-yet seen, is so critical. There are plenty of times when we get a brilliant idea and it temporarily fails or it pushes us into unfamiliar territory. If we don't have a strong connection to the truth—we live in an abundant Universe, we are awesome, glorious and tear-jerkingly lovable, etc.—a blazing desire, and an unflinching belief in our own vision before it's manifested, we'll fall prey to our own fears and everyone else's fears that it's not possible and give up, instead of course-correcting or pushing on through and bringing it to life. As Winston Churchill so aptly explained, "Success consists of going from failure to failure without loss of enthusiasm."

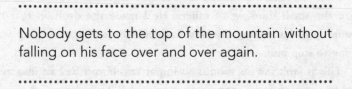

Nobody gets to the top of the mountain without falling on his face over and over again.

By the way, back when Henry Ford insisted to a roomful of annoyed engineers that his V-8 engine could be built the way he envisioned it, it was after he'd already gone bankrupt in his first attempt at creating an automobile empire. So at that time, he already had plenty of *proof* that he was capable of failing on a massive scale, but his faith in himself and his vision was so strong that he stuck with it, in spite of all the evidence around him that pointed to "big fat loser," and became one of the must successful entrepreneurs of all time.

Temporary failure is all the rage. All the cool kids have done it:

• Michael Jordan was cut from his high school basketball team for lack of skill.

• Steven Spielberg, a high school dropout, was rejected from film school three times.

• Thomas Edison, who was dubbed too stupid to learn anything by a teacher, tried more than nine thousand experiments before successfully creating the light bulb.

• Soichiro Honda, the founder of Honda Motor Company, was turned down by Toyota for an engineering position so he started his own damn company.

• Beethoven's music teacher told him he was talentless, and more specifically, was hopeless at composing. Beethoven turned a deaf ear. (I know, so bad. Sorry.)

• Fred Smith wrote a paper while at Yale about his big idea for an overnight delivery service. He got a C. He went on to create FedEx anyway.

••

The only failure is quitting. Everything else is just gathering information.

••

There's no big mystery to this stuff: If you want something badly enough and decide that you will get it, you will. You've done it before—you've lost the weight, gotten the job, bought the house, quit the nasty habit, gotten in shape, asked someone out, splurged on the front row tickets, grown out your bangs—you just need to remember that you can do it with anything in your life, *even the things that you presently think are out of your reach.*

There are plenty of people out there in the world living the kind of life you only dream about living, many of whom are far less fabulous and talented than you are. They key to their success is that they decided to go for it, they stopped listening to their tired old excuses, changed their lousy habits, and got the fuck on the fuck.

Here's how you can, too:

1. WANT IT BAD

You need to have a ten-ton gorilla of desire behind your decision or
else you'll wimp out the second things get hard. It's like people who
get hypnotized to quit smoking when they really don't want to quit, or
who try to lose weight when they're more excited by pizza than being
able to look down and see their feet. It never works. A few months ago
I dragged my ass to yoga class for a solid week even though I just so,
so, so did not feel like doing it. I paid my money, sat on my mat, and
was surprised to find my hand raised in the air when the instructor
asked if anyone had any injuries she should know about. I then heard
myself explaining that I'd just gotten the cast off my broken elbow and
should really take it easy. I am an adult. I am very busy. I spent money
on that class and then lied so I didn't have to participate. (I *did* have a
cast, but it had come off about eight months earlier.) I spent the
majority of Yoga Week quietly napping on my mat and conjuring up
my best "wincing in pain" face in case she was looking at me whilst I
was half-assing Down Dog. It was ridiculous.

If you're going to push through major obstacles to reach your goal,
you can't just want to want to; you need to be in a full-on tizzy of
excitement about what it is you're going after and hold on to it like a
pit bull. In order to do this you need to have the audacity to be honest about what you really want to do, not what you *should* do, believe
it's available to you regardless of any evidence otherwise, and go for it.

2. GET GOOD AT IT

To decide means literally *to cut off.* No wonder so many people are
totally freaked out by it! The terror around making the wrong decision
can be so overwhelming to some people that they develop the habit of

A) Waffling back and forth, paralyzed by self-doubt and terror, finally eeking out a "decision" that they then proceed to change over and over and over again B) Making decisions hastily, without thinking or feeling into them, their main goal being to escape the discomfort and get the damn thing over with already or C) Being so afraid that if they pick one thing, they'll miss out on another, so they either choose to do nothing or try to do everything, which are both excellent ways to miss out on all of it. They basically decide to never decide because they don't want to make the wrong decision. Good times!

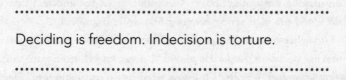

Deciding is freedom. Indecision is torture.

Indecision is one of the most popular tricks for staying stuck within the boundaries of what's safe and familiar. Which is why a common trait of successful people is that they make decisions quickly and change them slowly. And by quickly I don't mean that you must know exactly what to do the moment a decision presents itself (although there are those people who do), but rather that you immediately face the damn thing and start working through your decision-making process, whatever that may look like: sleeping on it, making a list of the pros and cons, feeling into it, etc.

If you're a waffler, or prefer to avoid the process altogether, a great thing to do is practice on the little things to build up your decision-making muscle. When eating at restaurants, make yourself pick something off the menu in under thirty seconds. Once you choose, you are unauthorized to change your mind or your order. Give yourself twenty minutes to go online and research the best garlic press and then make the purchase. Pick things off the shelves at the supermarket in under ten seconds. Knock yourself out of the habit of being a deer stuck in the headlights by demanding you wake up and choose something.

If you're someone who needs to sleep on it or mull it around a bit, give yourself a deadline. Don't leave it open until you decide and risk waking up forty years later, finally sure of what to do, long after the opportunity has passed you by. Pay attention to how much time you need to decide (overnight, a week, a month) and demand of yourself that you figure it out by then.

If you're wired for making instant decisions, practice tuning into your intuition and fully trusting what it says (regardless of what your brain may be screaming about). Get quiet, listen for and feel into the answer, and practice acting on your first, solid impulse.

And whoever you are, puhleeze, stop saying how pathetic you are at making decisions. Erase the phrase "I don't know," from your vocabulary and replace it with "I'll know what to do soon enough." Decide to become the person who makes quick, smart decisions and you will.

3. ELIMINATE THE NEGOTIATION PROCESS

When I decided to quit smoking, if I even toyed with thoughts like "Well, what harm will one itty-bitty drag do?" I was screwed. Our decisions must be watertight, because excuses will seep through any little cracks in our resolve and before we know it, we'll be on our asses.

· ·

Decisions are not up for negotiation.

· ·

The old you, the one who has not yet decided to kick ass, is in the past. Stay present and do not, even for a second, look backward or entertain any ideas of straying from your decision. Think only of the new you.

The whole point of deciding is to stop wasting time and to move forward, *not* to spend time figuring out how you can wiggle out of your decision! It helped me to think of it this way: I'm not going to go home and negotiate about whether or not I'm going to smoke a cigarette just as I'm not going to go home and negotiate about whether or not to snort some horse tranquilizers. I don't negotiate about snorting horse tranquilizers because I'm not a horse-tranquilizer snorter. Now that I don't smoke, I'm not going to negotiate about smoking because *I don't smoke.*

4. STICK LIKE GLUE

I used to write for an entrepreneurial magazine where I got to interview all these hugely successful business owners. Whenever I asked them what the secret to their success was, the overwhelming majority answered: Tenacity. Be the last person standing. Wear down your obstacles and excuses and fears and doubts until they're finally like, "You? Again? Jesus H. Christ, fine, here you go, now get out of my face."

Birthing your dreams is like. . . . giving birth. Conceiving the idea is the fun part (hopefully), then you go through insane amounts of fear and excitement and dreaming and planning and vomiting and growing and thinking you're crazy and thinking you're awesome and stretching and shape shifting until you're practically unrecognizable to everyone, even your own self. Along the way you clean up your puke and massage your aching back and apologize to all the people whose heads your ripped of in a hormonal killing spree, but you stay the course because you *know* this baby of yours is going to be *the bomb.* Then, finally, just when you can see a light at the end of the tunnel, labor starts. Your innards twist and strangle and force you to stumble around hunched over in the shape of the letter "C" while you breathe and pray and curse and just when you think it can't get any more out-of-your-mind painful, *a giant baby head squeezes out of a tiny hole in your body.*

Then. A full-blown miracle appears.

In order to change your life and start living a new one that you've never lived before, your faith in miracles, and yourself, must be greater than your fear. However easy or rough your birth process is, you have to be willing to fall down, get up, look stupid, cry, laugh, make a mess, clean it up and not stop until you get there. No matter what.

5. LOVE YOURSELF

You can do anything.

CHAPTER 24:

MONEY, YOUR NEW BEST FRIEND

I worked for a menial's hire
Only to learn, dismayed
That any wage I asked of Life
Life would have willingly paid.

—Anonymous

Many years ago, Los Angeles was hit by a relentless rainstorm the likes of which I'd never seen in my life. It rained for what seemed like forty days and forty nights, nonstop and hard. Rivers overflowed. Houses slid down hillsides. Bad hair wreaked chaos throughout the most image-conscious city in the world.

This was the kind of rain you didn't want to be driving around in in anything, let alone a twenty-three-year-old junker convertible with a leaky roof, no grill, a back window that was duct-taped shut and a front tire that went flat every three days.

I'd been in the market for a new car for a long time and couldn't find anything I really loved or thought I could afford, but as I sat there in a puddle, driving to the supermarket with a trash bag under my ass and an old T-shirt slammed in the door to keep the leaking to a minimum, it occurred to me that perhaps I should speed up my search.

At the time, I didn't have a whole lot of money, but I had my own business that I was trying to grow. The problem was I felt stuck in that place where even though I wanted bigger and better things for myself, monetarily, as well as feeling more mighty and self-actualized in general, I was worried that if I raised my prices I'd lose all my clients. And my self-respect. Or that I'd get called out as a money-grubbing pig. Or a fraud who had no right to charge that much. I was also scared that if I went big and grew my business, I wouldn't be able to handle it, I'd have to hire tons of people, I'd spend my time doing things I hated, I'd get so busy I'd never get to travel, I'd wither and die trapped behind my computer, fun and freedom skidding away in my rearview mirror never to be seen again blah, blah, blah. I could fill up about four more pages of reasons why I was where I was, but suffice it to say, I was basically playing at the level of someone who drives around in a car like the one I was driving around in.

And the most painful part really was that even though all signs pointed to Broke, Clueless, and Stuck, deep down I knew I could be doing SO much better. Which is why, even though the sound of crickets could be heard echoing throughout my empty bank account, I wandered into the Audi dealership, took the brand new Q5 for a spin and let the sales guy rattle on and on about leather this and premium that. In my head I was thinking, "Do you have any idea who I *am*? I'm just taking a fantasy break before heading over to Honda," but in my heart I knew better. Way down deep it was about much more than just a damn car.

It was about no longer being the kind of person who takes what she can get, and finally becoming the kind of person who creates exactly what she wants.

It was large, Marge. And because part of me was terrified to grow and part of me wanted to blast out and be huge, and also because I love to drive more than I love to eat, I tortured myself over which car to buy for weeks.

I finally whittled it down to two options:

The Honda CRV, a perfectly excellent little SUV with the following attributes:

- Okay gas mileage

- A sunroof

- Room for friends

- A comfy ride

- A ho-hum stereo

- Reasonably fun to drive

- Decently priced

Or:

The Audi Q5, a stick of butter on four wheels with the following attributes:

- Okay gas mileage

- A sunroof that takes up the entire roof of the car

- Room for friends—big, fat, and tall ones

- Leather seats you could have a sexual relationship with

- A stereo designed by God Himself

- Angels sing when you open the doors

- Sexy, flashy, expensive, pretentious, terrifying

I came very close to buying the Honda, but as I sat there, test-driving it for the tenth time, trying to convince myself that this was the One, I couldn't shake the nagging truth that I was in love with someone else. Buying the Honda would have been the sensible thing to do, but I knew that adventure, true love, and a whole new way of life awaited me on the other side of my comfort zone.

Blasting through this comfort zone is what I want to talk about here. Purchasing the Audi should have had me waking up screaming in the middle of the night because it cost the kind of money I would normally only consider spending on something like mandatory heart surgery, certainly not on something as frivolous as a car. But after I bought it I slept like a baby. Because once I made the decision to buy it, I also made the decision to get over my shit and become the kind of person who can make the kind of money to buy that kind of car or who can do anything else I want to do.

I almost instantly came up with a way to pay off the Audi and am certain that if I'd bought the Honda, I'd still be struggling to pay for it. Because I'd still be playing small, I'd still be in the mindset that I can't afford more, that I'm the kind of person who has to struggle to get whatever she can, that I can't break out of my mold and go get something completely "out of my reach," etc.

•••

When you up-level your idea of what's possible, and decide to really go for it, you open yourself up to the means to accomplish it as well.

•••

I'm not talking about going out and recklessly blowing all your money on stupid crap. I'm talking about *expanding your beliefs about what is available to you in all areas of your life.* And for the purposes of this chapter, I'm going to focus on what kind of money you believe is here for you to purchase the things and experiences you truly desire.

Whether or not the money is currently in your bank account is irrelevant (I didn't have the money either when I bought my new car). When you're available to play a bigger game, i.e. quit your ho-hum job and invest in your own business, buy a house, send your kids to private schools, hire a coach, hire a housecleaner, buy a new mattress, etc., you either need to pay for it with the money you have, or manifest the money if you don't have it already. And manifesting it is going to be pretty damn hard if you insist that not only is it not there for you, but that you aren't the kind of person who could ever make it or pay it off if you borrowed it.

In order to transform your life, you may have to spend the money you do have, get a loan, sell something, borrow from a friend, put it on your credit card, or manifest it in some other way. Which is going to go against some pretty deep-seated beliefs we've all been raised with about how going into debt is irresponsible (unless it's a student loan, of course, because for some reason we've decided in that case, and that case only, it's okay). This is about taking a leap of faith into a new realm *that you strongly desire to be in,* demanding of yourself that you rise to the occasion and start living your damn life already.

After I took my great leap into Luxury Carland, I made multiple six-figures with my business for the first time ever, began traveling the world on a regular basis, got my third book deal, made huge donations (for me) to causes I'm really passionate about, and helped my clients achieve similar personal bests, too.

Here's the thing: Making money isn't only about the money, just as losing weight isn't only about losing weight and finding your soul mate isn't only about finding your soul mate. It's about who you become and what you believe is possible for yourself.

Money is currency and currency is energy.

As we've discussed, we live in a Universe that is vibrating with energy. Our Universe is abundant, and everything you desire is here, in this moment, waiting for you to shift your perception and your energy and receive it. Money included.

Money is energy like anything else, and when you're operating at a high frequency with no resistance to it, and take right action, you can manifest the money you desire. We all know that we have to work to make money, we've been taught that all our lives, but what we're not taught is that we must also align our energy with the financial abundance we seek. In other words, act as if you're where you want to be, don't hang out with sad sacks and people who whine about how broke they are all the time, erase the words "I can't" from your vocabulary, envision what you desire, set goals, demand of yourself that you become who you need to become to create the life you desire. Our relationship to money is just as important as the action we take to manifest it, which is one reason why so many people who work their asses off their whole lives, but who have lousy energy around money, are left wondering why they have nothing to show for it.

Here's a little one-sided dialogue that may or may not sound familiar to you:

Yay! I think you're fun to hang out with too! Wait, what? You think I'm the root of all evil? How can you say that? All you talk about is how you wish you had more of me. Even though you're scared to admit you like me. And you say I'm not there for you. And you think people who like me are greedy pigs. Yet you get so ecstatic whenever I show up. And you work so hard to get me to come over. But I keep you in a constant state of worry. And you hate dealing with me.

And no matter what I do, it's never enough. One minute you act like you'll die without me, and the next I make you feel like a filthy whore. You know what? I'm done. See you later, freak.

Considering that this, or some version of this, is the sort of relationship most people have with money, I don't think the question is: "Why can't we make the kind of money we want?" I think the better question is: "How the hell do we expect to?" Most people have such conflicted feelings around money that they turn it into a full-on circus, rivaled only by the equally popular freak shows surrounding religion and sex. All three are crammed to the brim with issues and anxieties and staunch, fight-to-the-death beliefs that cause them to bring so much sadness to the world. Meanwhile, if everyone would just chill out, sex, money, and religion could be the leading causes of joy.

Silly, ain't we?

In order to bring money joyfully into our lives, we have to understand that we're having a relationship with it, and then treat it like any other important and meaningful relationship: we need to pay attention to it, want it, nurture it, put effort into it, respect it, cherish it, love it, etc.

Ridding yourself of your fear and loathing of money, be it conscious or subconscious, is essential if you want to make any. I was extremely poverty-proud for so long, I felt I was so much nobler in my pursuit of art and fun and altruism than those people who wasted their lives just going after money. No way in hell was I going to sacrifice my awesome life just to chase the filthy dollar! No, instead I was going to choose between having health insurance or a place to live. I was going to spend precious time (that I could have spent, uh, making money) driving an extra thirty blocks to the gas station where I could save three cents a gallon, sifting through piles of clothes in search of the gems at Goodwill, clipping coupons, hunting down sales, researching which bars had free food at happy hour, productive things like that. In my quest to make money an inconsequential part of my life, I was basically thinking about it more than anyone who actually had money ever thought about it.

What I didn't realize was that it's not an either/or situation. I could make great money and keep my integrity and have more fun and make more art and help more people and make a bigger difference in the world.

Oh.

I just had to get over myself. I had to stop working with the equation that wanting/having money = greedy scumbag. And I had to get a freakin' plan.

FIRST RULE OF WEALTH CONSCIOUSNESS: COME FROM A PLACE OF ABUNDANCE, NOT LACK

When we say we want money for something, we often come from a place of "I don't have it, it does not exist, so I need to create it." This has us focusing on, and believing in, lack, thereby lowering our frequency and attracting more lack.

When we say, "I am manifesting five grand to go on a trip to Italy you just watch me," our faith in the yet unseen is strong and our frequency is high. Thus, so is our ability to attract money. This is why buying the car worked so well for me—it forced me to face my fears and strengthen my faith because I bought it *before* I had proof that the money was there. *I don't see the money, but I believe it's there and it will be mine dammit!*

This abundance is available to everyone, including you, regardless of what your life looks like at this very moment. Some people are born into cushy lives full of trust funds and connections and opportunities and fancy educations; some of these people go on to make great financial successes of their lives and some of these people don't. Some people are born into extreme poverty and live in cardboard box houses by the side of a freeway; some of these people go on to make great financial successes of their lives and some of these people don't.

While their obstacles and initial childhood impressions about money can be extremely different, those who achieve success share one key thing: the belief that they can be, do, and have whatever they set their minds to accomplishing.

••

Your beliefs hold the key to your financial success.

••

Believe that you can have what you desire, that it really truly already exists, and then go out and get it. Once you understand that we live in an abundant Universe, you can also drop the limiting belief that you serve the world better by not taking too much for yourself or by getting too big. Your playing small simply withholds your gifts from the people who were meant to receive them, including you. Can you imagine if your favorite musicians never let themselves make enough money to buy guitars or take lessons or hire producers or buy purple platform boots and tight sparkly pants or pay thousands of dollars for studio time so they could record the songs that saved your ass in high school? Or if the people who build airplanes refused to make the money they need to pay for the research and the materials and the factories and the engineers and the electricity and whatever plethora of other costly things that go into building the miraculous flying machines that allow us to travel the world, hang out on tropical beaches, and visit the people we love so dearly?

The more you have, the more you have to share.

There's plenty of money to go around; you not letting yourself make it doesn't save more for other people just as you making it doesn't take it away from them. The only reason you should feel gross about accepting money for a product or service is if you're scamming someone (not doing or giving them what you said you would) or if you're causing harm in some other way. It's all about contributing to the world by making life easier, happier, safer, healthier, better, tastier, more beautiful, more fun, more interesting, more thoughtful, more loving—whatever you do, bring something good to the party. If you're coming from a place of integrity, any icky feelings you have about not deserving the wealth you desire are a waste of time. Just as any icky feelings you have about money itself are a waste of time. Greedy people do greedy things for money, so don't go getting all up in money's face and blame it for their lousy behavior.

Here's a brilliant little spanking in this department from author/ speaker, Marianne Williamson, that I recently heard in a talk she gave:

"Having money is like anything else; a tool. And if you see it that way, making it not just about you, but about a way that you can play a part in the dynamic by which money is used for the betterment of all things, then having money is not only a blessing, it's a responsibility."

Having money is a responsibility! Let your inner money critic chew on *that* one for a while.

SECOND RULE OF WEALTH CONSCIOUSNESS: GET CLEAR ON WHERE YOU'RE AT

Write a little ditty on how you feel about money. Get clear on all your craziness around it because trust me, if you don't have any money, you definitely have some crazy. Write something along the lines of:

So the truth is I don't really trust money. I want lots of it so I can do whatever I want and make big changes in the world, but I don't believe it will come to me. Or that if it does, it won't stick around. It never has. I resent needing it. I think people who make it are evil and have bad priorities. I ignore it because I hate dealing with it. I wouldn't know what to do with it if I made it anyway. If it's easier, pretend money is a person and write it as if you're writing a letter to someone. Just get it on the page so you can look at it.

Then break it down, sentence by sentence and expose your drama around money for the award-winning performance that it is. For example, using the paragraph above:

I don't believe money will come to me. Has it ever? I guess so. Can you imagine a specific time and a specific amount that came to you that was really helpful and enjoyable? *Yes. I was a graphic designer for five years. I got to work on a lot of really cool projects with great people making good money.* Any other times? Have you had other jobs or monetary gifts or dividends? *Yes.* Can you list off five to ten significant times that money came to you? *Okay.* So if it came to you all these many times, is it possible that it could come to you again? *Yeah.* Can you change your belief from, "Money doesn't come to me" to, "Money does come to me?" *Fine. Yes I can.*

Now that you see the truth, focus on money coming to you, imagine receiving all the money you need, visualize how you'll spend it and *feel* it in your bones. Change your story from "Money doesn't come to me," to "Money comes to me all the time." Make this an affirmation that you walk around saying in your mind and out loud, that you write down, read over and over, and tape to your bathroom mirror, etc. Drill it into your brain and your bones.

Another example:

I resent needing it. How come? *Because I never have enough to do what I want.* Is this true? Have you never had enough money to do what you want? *Well, there have been some times where I've had the money.* So is it true that you never have enough money to do what you want? *No.* And when you have the money you need to do what you want, do you resent needing it? *Not really.* How does it feel when you have it and you spend it on something you're really excited about buying for you or someone else? *Pretty cool actually.* So is it true you resent needing it? *No.*

Once you've caught yourself in your big fat lie, focus on spending money lavishly on yourself or the people you love or a cause you're passionate about or whatever and *feel* it in your bones. Imagine receiving it and feel yourself filling up with gratitude for it coming to you. Be grateful to money for the awesome tool it is and for allowing you to feel so good. Replace your story that "I resent needing money" with "I'm grateful to money for helping me live such an awesome life."

Start healing your relationship with money. Sit your broke ass down and write a letter to money and then break it down, sentence by sentence like I just did above (really DO this please), and create some new money affirmations. Repeat your new affirmations and feel them in your bones. Walk around thinking about how much you love, love, love money. (Did reading that just make you throw up in your mouth a little bit?)

You are going against some seriously deeply-ingrained beliefs here; money is incredibly loaded for most people, so if you want to get over your issues and start making money, *spend time on this.* You are rewriting a story that was written in blood, by you and generations before you, that you've been buying into in your whole life, so it's going to take some effort to rewrite it and start living it.

THIRD RULE OF WEALTH CONSCIOUSNESS: GET CLEAR ON WHERE YOU DESIRE TO BE

We all need money. We need it to feed ourselves, buy clothes, get shelter, water, medicine, etc. Once it goes beyond basic survival, however, and we get into the arena of how much money we "need," if we've got guilt and judgment and terror over what it means to have it and what people will think of us if we do, this is where all hell is gonna break loose.

Of course, none of us "need" more than the basics to survive, but if we're talking about blossoming into the fullest expressions of our best selves in an abundant Universe, we do. Which is why, I'm assuming, you're reading this book instead of one on how to distinguish edible berries from poisonous ones. You don't want to merely survive, you want to *thrive* in every area of your life, including the area of financial support.

Being wealthy means having the resources to provide yourself with everything you need, and desire, to share your gifts with the world as your biggest, badassiset self. This means being wealthy psychologically, spiritually, and energetically as well as materially. Let's say you've got your own clothing company. You need money to have a space to create your designs, you need to pay for materials, manufacturing, shipping, payroll, marketing, and all the other expenses of running your business.

That's obvious. But you also need to feel healthy, happy, and good so you can do your best work and bring the most awesome products to your customers. Maybe you need to live and work in a place you love that inspires you or hire assistants so you're not exhausted and spread thin or do things that fill you with happiness like travel and buy your friends dinner or join a gym or get a puppy or buy clown noses for everyone in your office. Maybe you want to give twenty percent of your income to help drill water wells in Africa as well as hire more staff so you can donate some time to doing charity work. It ALL counts. Feeling like you don't deserve the things that make you the happiest and best version of yourself, because it's greedy or is asking too much, ultimately rips off the rest of the world because you aren't being fully supported and, as a result, aren't sharing your highest frequency with the world.

Be your best, do your best, demand the best, expect the best, receive the best, and put your best out into the world so everyone can receive your best, too.

Think of it this way: would you rather hang out in a world where everyone feels happy and well taken care of and aspires to be the best they can be or be, or would you rather be in a world where people live in fear and shame and scrimp and hold themselves back? What would each scenario do to *your* energy?

> One of the best things you can do to improve the world is to improve yourself.

It's a grassroots effort. So if you need money to improve your life, get over it already and go get yourself some. 'Cuz this isn't just about you, m'kay?

In order to go get some money, get very clear on what kind of life will make you truly happy. And be honest. What kind of experiences and possessions will support you in the work you want to do and in the kind of life you'd love to live? If you're truly happy living a simple life in a yurt surrounded by people you love, trading little trinkets you've carved out of cow bones for food and making just enough to get by, that's one thing, but pretending you don't want more than you already have because you can't afford it or feel guilty and pretentious for wanting it—that's another. That is called being a weenie. Determine what your, personal, truest version of success looks like (no comparing yourself to others please), figure out how much it will cost, and then set out with steadfast determination to manifest the money you need to create it.

FOURTH RULE OF WEALTH CONSCIOUSNESS: RAISE YOUR FREQUENCY

Money on its own means nothing. A one-hundred-dollar bill sitting on a table is a piece of paper. It's the energy around it that makes it relevant. That one one-hundred-dollar could have been slipped into a birthday card from your granny or you could have stolen it from your best friend when she wasn't looking or you could have earned it by doing something you loved or by doing something you hated. In each situation, the energy around the money is different.

Nothing has any value other than the value we put on it.

Similarly, the monetary value we put on things and services has energy. Someone could sell a T-shirt in a store for ten dollars. Another person could sell the exact same T-shirt in some fancy store for one thousand dollars. How much is a gold watch worth? How much is a broken watch worth that was owned by Michael Jackson?

It's all make-believe. Or rather, *it's all what we make ourselves believe.* If we believe we are worth ten dollars an hour, that's the frequency we'll put out and that's the kind of client or job we'll attract. If we believe we're worth one thousand dollars an hour, that's the frequency we'll put out and that's the kind of client or employment opportunities we'll attract. They key word is believe—you can't be shitting bricks and charging more than you believe you're worth and expect to receive it, and you can't charge less than you believe you're worth and expect to flourish because you'll be pissed off.

In order to create wealth, you must bring yourself into energetic alignment with the money you desire to manifest.

Three people can do the same thing for a living, let's say they're chiropractors for example. One makes fifty thousand a year, one makes one hundred thousand a year, one makes one million dollars a year. Is the guy who makes a million dollars *that* much better than the guy who makes fifty thousand? And how do you put a price tag on his betterness? Is the way he cracks someone's back nine hundred and fifty thousand dollars a year times better than the guy who makes fifty thousand dollars? He may be more skilled or have more experience (but then again, he may not), but what it ultimately comes down to is his decision of his worth. He is operating at a one-million-dollar frequency so that's what he's charging. And getting.

• •

Money is an exchange of energy between people.

• •

When you charge your clients from a certain frequency or demand a certain salary, you attract clients and employers who are already at that frequency. You're not putting a gun to their heads. You are not the only person offering these goods and services; they're free to work with or hire someone who's at a different frequency than you are, but they're coming to you. And part of what you offer is the opportunity to meet at your frequency. By lowering your frequency out of fear leaves everyone vibrating at a lower frequency.

If it's important to you to offer your services for free or rock-bottom prices for people in serious deep doo-doo, then you can have a charitable leg of your business or some sort of scholarship dealio or find a patron or get grants or seek another means of income that sustains you while you work for free. But exhausting yourself because you need to work eight million hours in order to survive because you feel guilty charging what you're worth is real low-level stuff. You ultimately wind up helping fewer people because you're tired and crabby and less effective.

So, where are you at energetically with what you make? And where do you want to be?

You can figure this out by getting nice and clear on the kind of life you desire to live, figuring out what you need to be making to manifest this reality and set about matching your frequency to your desired income. If you're nowhere near where you want to be, keep pushing yourself to raise your prices or seek higher paying jobs. Surround yourself with higher frequency experiences and people. Beef up your education and know-how. Make vision boards of what you want your life to look like. Again, raising your frequency is like developing a muscle—strengthening it is a process.

FIFTH RULE OF WEALTH CONSCIOUSNESS: STAY IN SHAPE

You must keep your frequency high and your belief in limitless possibility strong to manifest your dream house or your goal of going to the Olympics or to call in your soul mate. Otherwise you run the risk of sliding backward into having your father's lame relationship with money or your mother's terror of being visible or your divorced parents' mistrust of intimacy. When it comes to being mighty about money, one of the best ways to do this is to read wealth consciousness books. All the time. Over and over. My two staples have always been *Think and Grow Rich* by Napoleon Hill and *The Science of Getting Rich* by Wallace Wattles (listed in the back of this book), but there are plenty others out there. Find some that work for you and read them for at least thirty minutes every single day. Surround yourself with inspiring people who don't think money is bad and those who either already have it or are intent on making it. Watch your thoughts and your words. Make a conscious effort to keep your positive financial mind-set strong and unwavering.

GET INTO REALITY ABOUT HOW MUCH YOU WANT TO MAKE AND WHY

There are countless ways to make serious money, and depending on what business you're in they will obviously vary, but there are some general rules that apply across the board. Start by thinking about the life you'd love to live and why, figure out exactly how much money you need to manifest to make it happen. If you don't know how much it would cost to build your dream house, do the research. If you want to travel, figure out where and by when and do the math on exactly how much it all will cost. If you want a lifestyle where you eat out more and wear nicer clothes, crunch the numbers. How much money do you now need to make per year? Per month? Per hour? The Universe responds to details. The Universe responds to energy. The Universe responds to badasses.

There is a big difference between walking around saying you want to make a million dollars a year, and having crystal clear intentions, fierce desire, and hell-bent action toward specific goals.

Make a list, be super specific about exactly what it is, how much it will cost, why you want it, how it will make you feel, etc. You need to be in a full-on lather about it and want it so badly that it is not negotiable: It will and it must happen regardless of how long it takes. Decide what it is you want and write down the exact cost.

MAKE IT URGENT

Ever notice how when your rent is due in a week and you have no idea how you're going to pay it, or if you really need a specific amount of money for a specific urgent purpose like getting a throbber of a rotten tooth pulled, that you always manage to somehow figure out how to get the money just in time? Usually a check that you had forgotten about arrives in the mail or an unexpected freelance job comes in or you suddenly develop the nerve to ask somebody for a loan or you sell grandma's jewelry or you compete with the five-year-old selling lemonade down the street and make a killing. You shift from wasting your time whining and worrying because you're suddenly too busy making it happen. This is the power of:

- Clarity

- Urgency

- Not screwing around

The money is there if you really, truly desire it. It's just a matter of being so serious about it that you don't stray from the path of manifesting it no matter what gets thrown in it.

The trick is to treat your dreams with this same urgency and determination. It's one thing to kick ass when your back is against the wall and you've got to come up with your kid's tuition, and quite another to create self-imposed urgency so you stay the course until you've created your dream life instead of settling back into the Big Snooze. You need a sense of urgency to keep from dropping the ball when it gets difficult and sliding down into thinking, "Ah, screw it, I'm fine living next door to a kennel full of barking dogs. It's nothing getting some earplugs and boarding up my windows can't fix." Instead of being in reaction mode, it's about being in action mode. It's about no longer acting like a victim (letting your circumstances control your life) and instead acting like a superhero (creating a life that has you waking up in giddy disbelief that you get to be you).

A great way to psyche yourself into up-leveling is by raising your bottom line. So often we take the massive leaps of faith only when we have to, when we need to put out some sort of fire aka pay off some huge bill. Because this is about changing *you*, not just about changing your income, why not decide to be the kind of person who always has a certain amount of money in the bank? Be someone who's not in struggle and panic and constantly behind the eight ball. Come up with a figure and decide your account will never go below it. Make it non-negotiable. For example, if you decide that you will always have two thousand dollars in your checking account and refuse to see your balance go under it, it will light the fire under your ass to generate income the second you get close to dipping below it. Or decide that you will always donate ten percent of what you make to charity, no matter what. Make a new bottom line; get yourself out of struggle by changing your mind-set and being conscious of how you deal with, generate, and receive your money.

ENVISION YOURSELF WITH THIS MONEY AND THE SPECIFIC THINGS AND/OR EXPERIENCES IT'S GOING TO PROVIDE

As I said, money on its own means nothing. It's what we attach to it that gives it meaning and inspires us to have it in our lives. It's what this money makes us feel like that puts us in the proper tizzy to manifest it. Write a mantra that you can run over and over in your mind to help you manifest the money you desire. *I see myself making $150,000 by December 31st by being an accountant and serving thirty new clients in the best way possible. I'm so grateful for this $150,000 by December 31st that allows me to take my family on a vacation to Bali and renovate our kitchen and donate money to build schools in Kenya. I see myself in the jungle with my kids and my wife; we're staying at my favorite hotel in Ubud. I feel so happy for being able to give my children this incredible, life-changing experience and for bringing my wife such joy. I can also see the kitchen and how happy it's made my wife to finally have it. I see the faces of the kids in Kenya as write on the chalkboard in the school I've helped pay for. I feel such joy from being able to make a difference in their lives. I'm so grateful for this $150,000 that I will make by December 31st. I see the awesome clients I get to work with who are more than happy to pay me $100 an hour for my services. This money is mine, it is on its way to me now, I see it in my bank account and am so grateful for it.*

Write one that makes you feel invincible, read it over and over every day, see it and feel it and become a crazy person about it. I know, this sounds like a pain in the ass, but do it anyway because, trust me, it works. Lame, vague goals are the best way to live a lame, vague life. If you want to knock it out of the park, you need to know exactly what you're shooting for. And be so excited about it that you're almost annoying to yourself.

TAKE HELL-BENT-FOR-GLORY ACTION

Do every single thing you can think of to manifest this money/new lifestyle. If you've got your own business, what new programs could you offer or what new products could you sell? Can you raise your prices? Leverage your time? Sign on bigger and fancier clients? Sell more to the clients you already have? Pick up a part-time job? If you work for someone else, ask for a raise or look for a new job that pays more. Listen to everyone around you with new ears. Is there an opportunity for a new, better paying situation there that you may have not noticed before? Is there a position you can create or suggest that would get you at your desired income level? Continue to do everything humanly possible to magnetize it to you, and then surrender to The Universe and be on the lookout for something unexpected to come in: an inheritance, someone who wants to pay you for your expertise, a brilliant idea that you'd normally pass over as too out of the question, or a conversation between two people looking for someone just like you to help redesign their new offices. Look for some opportunity or person to make an appearance that's not in your usual path of income. You are leaping into a new reality here—it's not your job to know the *how*; it's your job to ask for what you want and wait to discover the *how*, then take action.

When the unexpected money or the new job or the big client comes in is up to The Universe. It can literally happen immediately or it can take years. Your job is to do everything you can to manifest it and have unshakable faith that the Universe is moving it toward you in perfect timing.

GET MENTORING

Surround yourself with people who know more than you do. Read
about them, study them, hang out with them and hire them. Be on the
lookout for the perfect coach or mentor or book or seminar, because
when the student is ready, the teacher appears. Pay attention to who
and what flies in your radar and learn as much as you can from them.

Love Yourself

And you will have it all.

CHAPTER 25:

REMEMBER TO SURRENDER

*Surrender to what is. Say "yes" to life and see how life suddenly
starts working for you, rather than against you.*
— **Eckhart Tolle; author, channeler, high priest of being present**

Imagine yourself sitting by a window, looking out at a garden on a
lovely spring day. You see birds and bees and butterflies merrily flitting
about, when all of a sudden, the most beautiful butterfly in the world
catches your eye. Its stunning turquoise wings make your heart
explode, its joyful flight makes your soul sing, its metamorphosis from
wet wormy thing to creature of soaring beauty fills you with inspiration. Suddenly you leap up, overcome and crazed with a fierce desire;
it must be mine mine mine! You sprint to the closet, grab your net, sneak
outside and tiptoe through the tulips, stalking your beloved prey, all
senses alert, focused, determined, tenacious, swinging your net over
your head as you chase your butterfly around the garden. You chase it

for hours and hours, but all you seem to be able to do is scare it off, rather than catch it. It's only when you stop trying so desperately, relax, breathe, and surrender your desire to The Universe that the butterfly of your dreams calmly comes and lands on your nose.

When we want something so, so badly and are working tirelessly to get it, if we don't surrender, we end up pushing it away instead. There comes a point where we need to hand the job over to The Universe. This doesn't mean that we give up or discontinue taking action. This means we let go *energetically,* release our kung fu grip and create some space for what we want to come to us. It's about allowing instead of forcing. It's about releasing and trusting that if it's in alignment with our life's purpose, it will come back to us (or that something or someone even more perfect will come in its place). It's about surrendering and letting The Universe do its thing while holding faith that our highest desire will come into our lives.

••

Your faith in The Universe must be stronger than your fear of not getting what you want.

••

It's like hiring someone to clean your house so you can focus on the other work you enjoy doing. You explain in detail what they're supposed to do, show them where the broom is, tell them you'll beat them to death if they break the ceramic mugs your niece made for you, but you trust them with the job. If you're constantly hovering over them and grabbing the sponge out of their hands—*here, let me do that!*—they'll never get their work done and you'll stay in overwhelmed struggle, preventing yourself from reaping the benefits that inspired you to hire your cleaning crew in the first place.

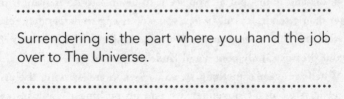

Surrendering is the part where you hand the job over to The Universe.

What often happens is that, regardless of our best intentions and hard work, we're trying to control our circumstances by using our limiting beliefs and old patterns. We think that we need to try and *take charge* of the situation (fear based thinking) instead of having faith and gratitude and *allowing* The Universe to deliver (love based thinking). In short, we think we can do a better job of manifesting than The Universe can.

Imagine that someone invites you to a party. They're all excited about their big old rager, are fully certain that it's going to be awesome and are truly delighted by the thought of having you come. They extend the invite with much glee and merriment and a deep desire to see you there but with zero pressure—they know if you come it will be awesome, they know if you don't come it will be awesome. Their party is going to rock. They believe this in their hearts. It is the truth.

Now imagine that someone else invites you to a different party. This person demands that you come, acts like their party will be a gigantic failure unless you show up and reminds you that they came to your last party so you have to come to theirs. They are whiney, manipulative, controlling, a big fat drag. They know they can have an awesome party, and really believe they can, but have decided that it all depends on you coming.

Both people can do the same exact things to prepare: decorate their houses, buy the cheese plates, get the booze, order the ice sculptures, but one person is much more likely to manifest what they want—you showing up and actually wanting to be there—than the other because they have surrendered. Surrendering isn't about what you do, but who you're being as you do it.

Your life is your party. You get to choose how you invite people and experiences and things into it.

If you're broke as a joke, it's not about working until you're half dead to make ends meet and whining about your pathetic situation. It's about showing up everyday with an excellent attitude, doing your best, leaning back, celebrating what is and steadily working with the grateful expectation and belief that The Universe is sending you a new, more lucrative opportunity.

If you're single, it's not about boo-hooing the fact that you can't find someone good or half-heartedly forcing yourself to go on a million dates. It's about keeping your desire strong and your faith unwavering, brushing your hair and teeth, leaving the house, flirting your ass off, joyfully going about your life and being grateful that not only is the person you're seeking also seeking you, but that The Universe is conspiring to bring you together.

Doubt is resistance, faith is surrender. Worry is resistance, joy is surrender. Control is resistance, allowing is surrender. Ridicule is resistance, believing is surrender.

Energy needs to flow or else it stagnates. Surrendering puts you in the flow.

Not only does surrendering create the space to manifest your desires, but it opens you up to manifest good feeling experiences and things that are presently outside your realm of awareness (a.k.a miracles).

As I mentioned before, when you're moving into a new, awesome life that you've never lived in before, you can't expect to know *how* to get there because it's new territory, so you can only do that which you already know how to do and stay open to discovering the new *how*. Likewise, you need to be open to the fact that you may not know exactly what your new reality will look like because you've never seen it before. You're only able to envision that which is already known to you, so the mind-bogglingly awesome new life may be out of your scope of imagination, and by stubbornly holding on to the exact vision of what you want instead of surrendering, you set yourself up to miss out entirely on the very thing you're looking for. Sometimes your new reality will look just as you pictured it, sometimes totally different (and way better).

Here's the basic breakdown on how to surrender:

- Get crystal clear on what you desire to manifest

- See it, feel it, taste it, fall in love with it, believe it is already here

- Decide you will have it

- Inform The Universe of your intention by behaving and thinking *as if you already have it*

- Meditate, connect with infinite possibility, your intuition and Source Energy

- Take hell-bent joyful, passion-fueled action

- Be grateful that it's yours, that it's already here

- Breathe, let it go, let it in

When you believe that everything you desire already exists, you are in a natural state of surrender.

Surrendering is the free-falling backwards into the unknown and trusting that The Universe will catch you. And this can't be done from a place of lack or a place of mistrust—*OK, I'm releasing, you better come through beotch!*—you have to give it all you've got and totally let it go for reals, you must fall back, have faith, be grateful, and wait. And while you're at it . . .

Love Yourself

And the Motherlode shall bestow her magic upon you.

CHAPTER 26:

DOING VS. SPEWING

God will not have his work made manifest by cowards.
—Ralph Waldo Emerson; fearless writer/poet, highly-
skilled spewer and doer

I have a friend who had the word "Duh" tattooed on the inside of her upper arm in homage to the fact that all of our big ah-ha moments are no-brainers; "Fear is a choice!" "I am lovable!" "Don't worry, be happy!" Every time she high-fives, or lifts her arm to see if she needs a shave, she gets reminded of how often the sublime lies waiting in the obvious.

You know countless of these truisms of which I speak, you've heard them or thought them a million times, but when they finally sink in and you "get it," they suddenly become earth-shattering news.

••

An epiphany is a visceral understanding of something you already know.

••

Once something moves from our brains to our bones, that's when
we can use it to change our lives.

The million-dollar question is, will we?

Oh, the years people spend talking the talk, rolling out the shoulds,
woulds and coulds, attending classes, trolling the seminar circuit, and
burying themselves in all sorts of shelf-helpery before they finally, if
ever, DO anything with it all.

There's a statistic that says only 5 percent of people who sign up
for something, like a course or a seminar, actually do anything with it.
And this includes very, very, very high-priced somethings, not just the
money-management class at the community college down the road.
This is because lots of people wish for change, really, really want it, are
willing to invest the time and money into it, but are ultimately not
willing to get uncomfortable enough to actually make anything happen. Which means they don't want it as badly as they say they do.

••

"I tried" is the poor man's "I kicked butt."

••

People who are successful are not only willing to get uncomfortable, but they know they have to make a habit of it if they want to stay
successful. They keep moving through each new challenge instead of
stagnating and settling. The muscle of kick-assery is like any other
muscle—you have to use it or lose it. If you have one big breakthrough

and feel like, *I got this, I am ON it,* and then sit back and wait for your long overdue stream of awesomeness to keep pouring in, you will lose your muscle mass and fall back to the marshmallow state that you were in before you started working out.

Keep moving, keep growing, keep pushing through obstacles, keep evolving. You break through at one level, arrive at the next, and take another step up. Each time you grow, you get to learn something new, which basically means you have to get uncomfortable again. Because when you arrive at a level you've never been at before, you're faced with challenges you've never experienced before. It's the willingness to keep pushing through new challenges, not shrink from them back into your comfort zone, that separates the successful from the unsuccessful.

New level, new devil.

All life is either moving forward and evolving or shrinking back and dying. If you want to evolve in your own life, you have to push through the obstacles instead of running from them. *Obstacles and challenges are the agents of growth.* Nobody gets to be large and in charge without facing challenges and moving through them. Birth is messy, painful, scary, uncertain, and freaky. Birth is also a glorious miracle that leads to new life. If you want the new life you say you want, you have to do the work instead of just studying and discussing and wishing and wanting.

I recently had a real wake-up call in this department that I'll share with you in hopes that it'll inspire you to do the work and keep the faith no matter what. At the moment I don't live anywhere, or I guess you could say I live everywhere. I got rid of my place two years ago and have been exploring the world indefinitely ever since. I've always loved traveling, and since all I need to run my business is my computer, a strong Internet connection, good cell phone reception and a sandwich, I decided to put all my things into storage and go for it. I saw this as a chance to walk my talk of living life on your own terms, to be the priestess of high vibe, to quantum leapfrog around the globe, to see in how many different languages I can learn how to say, "Would you mind watching my stuff while I go to the bathroom?"

My main focus at the moment is mastering Surrender. I want to have unshakable faith in the not-yet seen. I want to get so comfortable trusting The Universe that it becomes second nature and I can just leap into the void with toes pointed and daisy petals in my wake. Or, you know, at least do it with more grace and ease. Especially now that I'm traipsing around the world, loftily preaching about Decision this and Let it Go that.

I too would very much like to do instead of spew.

Surrender comes into play often, especially when it comes to figuring out where I'm off to next and where I'm going to stay once I get there. My modus operandi is to go with the flow and trust that The Universe will guide me to the perfect place at the perfect time, which, I'm quite pleased to report, has yet to disappoint: After following my sudden, and bizarre impulse to go to Tokyo (a city I had zero interest in checking out), I not only totally fell in love with the place, but the ideal furnished apartment came up for rent, and was handed to me on a silver platter, when I decided I wanted to live there for a while; An invitation to stay in a gorgeous guest house in the Spanish countryside with great friends came in, unsolicited and out of the blue, when I was trying, and failing, to figure out where to go next; I keep finding myself repeatedly, and fully coincidentally, crossing paths in distant corners of the world with several of my fellow, global nomads whom I met, and befriended, in Bali, and who have me drop-jawed and giddy every time I bump into them; *you're in a tiny, remote, fishing village wearing nothing but a sarong and a frizzy hairdo in the middle of nowhere Indonesia too?*

Yet even though my cosmic travel agent has more than proven that she knows exactly what she's doing, I was still fairly nervous about this last free-fall. Because this time it wasn't all, *Just send me anywhere that seems cool where awesome things will happen to me, m'kay? Thanks.* I needed to land in the perfect place to write this book. I only had a month left before it was due to the publisher and I had, um, quite a bit left of it to write, so I was a tad uptight about the wheres and the whats and the hows. I was in Tokyo at the time, and my plan was to fly to L.A. to meet with a client, then road trip through the American west and wind up at some fabulous, fully-furnished luxury rental home with a great view and lots of sunshine where I could concentrate and get lots of work done. I imagined being surrounded by awe-inspiring nature, but being close enough to a city where some friends lived in order to avoid the isolation best known for driving writers to drink heavily or, in my case, to delve into failed experiments with cutting my own hair. If there were animals around to keep me company, that would be the cherry on top, but the rest was non-negotiable.

About two weeks before leaving, I went online and started searching for houses to rent. I looked in every state west of Colorado, but everything I liked was booked. I asked everyone I knew and everyone I didn't know if they had any ideas; I sent out emails, Facebooked, Tweeted, and texted, but again, nothing. There was always the hotel option, but I really had my heart set on a house, and I was starting to panic about the fact that I'd waited until the last minute. This was a big deal—this was my book! I needed inspiration and high frequency! I wanted to look up from my desk and gaze out the window upon an awe-inspiring view of mountains or ocean or rolling fields! Meanwhile, if something didn't come through soon, I was going to be gazing out the window of the bedroom I grew up in upon my mother sweeping the driveway in her slippers.

I began resigning myself to the fact that I'd blown it. Instead of having faith in The Universe and joyously anticipating the manifestation of my dream home, I started shrinking and talking myself into taking what I could get. *What am I whining about? I'm lucky to have my mom's house to go to. I love her. Plus she'll feed me lasagna while I'm writing.* Then I realized what I was doing. What kind of hypocrite would I be if I got all fearful, small-minded, and low-vibe about where to write my book about how not to go through life fearful, small-minded, and low-vibe?

....

You have to keep the faith, always, even when your ass is on the line.

....

So, forty-eight hours before my flight left Tokyo for L.A., I calmly sat back, focused on my ideal writing palace, envisioned the wide open space it looked out upon, luxuriated in its plush couches and big open kitchen, soaked up the sun pouring in through its huge windows, felt it in my bones, believed it was real, did the whole wickety-woo thing, and got all excited and grateful that it already existed and was on its way to me. Then I sent out one more mass e-mail asking if anyone knew of a great place for me to write my book, surrendered it up to The Universe, and took myself out for a big fat sushi dinner to celebrate the awesome writing paradise that was about to land in my lap. When I returned to my hotel, there was an e-mail waiting for me from a friend who knew some people who had a place I could move into ASAP.

I'm pleased to report that I'm writing this in a big, luxurious, open, sunny, magnificent house with huge windows and spectacular views an hour outside of San Francisco where five of my best friends from college live. The house is on top of a hill overlooking seventeen acres of rolling farmland, and I can stay for as long as I want, as long as I take care of their adorable horse and two goats.

This. Shit. Works.

So, how serious are you about not settling? You can make a quantum leap in your life right now. You can change your entire reality on a dime if you want to badly enough or massively increase your income level or drop ten pounds or begin waking up excited to be who you are instead of merely putting up with your day until it's cocktail hour. Whatever level of upgrade you want, it's available to you, right now.

You just have to decide to make it happen, to be engaged with your life and let the Universe work for you.

Here are some ways to take what you've learned in this book and seal the deal:

1. GIVE YOUR BAD HABITS THE HEAVE-HO

Successful people have good habits; unsuccessful people have losery habits. Because our habits are all the things that we do automatically, without thinking, they help to define who we are: if you're in the habit of getting up and working out every morning, you're in shape; if you're in the habit of never doing what you say you're going to do, you're unreliable; and if you're in the habit of getting massages three times a week, you're really psyched.

Pay attention to the areas of your life that you're not so thrilled about, figure out which bad habits helped create them and trade those habits in for some good ones. Form the kind of habits that successful people have: good time-management habits, good decision-making habits, good thought habits, good health habits, good relationship habits, good work habits, etc. Think of what behaviors would make the biggest, positive changes in your life (maybe even the kinds of changes you can hardly imagine coming true) and set about turning them into habits.

How do you form a habit? Decide to. Make it a part of your regular, everyday activities. Make it as non-negotiable and thoughtless as brushing your teeth or getting out of bed. Schedule it in. Work on uncovering your subconscious beliefs and rewriting your stories. And if it's something you've tried and tried to change on your own, get some help. Hire a coach, a mentor, a personal trainer, tell a friend to spray paint "I am a lazy lard ass" on the side of your house if you don't reach your goal of going to the gym five days a week. Whatever you have to do, start developing successful habits if you want to become a successful person.

2. BREATHE AMONGST THE PEOPLE

Your superhero power, i.e. your connection to Source Energy, is available to you 24/7, not only when you're sitting cross-legged in your robe meditating. Once you get your brain used to shutting up and tuning into Source Energy, you can start doing it throughout your day.

The whole point of everything you've learned in this book is to use it to improve your life, not to take a break, go off and read, and then head back out to live your life again and leave everything you've learned back there, on the couch, where you were reading. You want to carry all the stress-relieving, life-appreciating, joy-delivering, mood-lifting, Source-connecting, butt-kicking benefits with you all day long. And the best way to do this is through your breath.

When you're stuck in traffic, getting yelled at by your boss, feeling awkward at a party, strolling through the office, lying on the beach, trying to remember how to get to your sister's house, take a moment to breathe deeply, clear your mind, check in with your bod, become present in the moment and connect with Source Energy.

The more of a habit you make this throughout your day, the more you will see profound, positive changes in your life both emotionally and physically, and the more gracefully you will be able to deal with

the next inconsiderate jerk who decides to yell into their cell phone
while sitting next to you at a restaurant.

3. HANG HIGH

Hang out with people who are kicking ass and who will make you feel
like a giant loser if you're not kicking ass, too. I (obviously) can't stress
this enough. Who you surround yourself with greatly affects how you
see your world and how high you set the bar for yourself. If you hang
out with people who constantly whine about how tired, broke and
worried about the economy they are, you'll feel like a hero just for
getting out of bed in the morning. Hang out with people who are living on purpose, who meet their challenges with a *step aside, suckers*
attitude, who are dating super awesome people, making exactly the
kind of money they want to be making (or working toward it) or taking the kinds of vacations they, and you, want to be taking, and you'll
not only see what's possible for you, too, but you'll have more incen-
tive to follow suit.

4. SET HONEST GOALS

Don't decide you're going to run ten miles a day when you still consider walking to the pizza parlor around the corner a day's worth of
exercise. Start with running half a mile a day and add more as you get
stronger. Discipline is a muscle; you have to build it at your own pace.
If you bite off more than you can chew at the start, chances are excellent you'll get discouraged and give up altogether. Set honest goals that
are just outside your comfort zone and build from there.

5. READ YOUR MANIFESTO

Write down your goals and your vision of your ideal life in the present tense and be as specific as possible. Where do you live, who do you live with, what do you do for fun, who are you surrounded by, how much money do you make, how do you make it, how do you give back to the world, what are you wearing, etc. Make it so freaking awesome that you can't read it without weeping and wailing and putting it down to compose yourself every few sentences. Read it to yourself before you go to bed and when you wake up every single solitary day *I am so not kidding over here*. Become obsessed with it. Think about how you're changing your life and who you're becoming and be in a state of giddy expectation about it as often as possible. The more you focus on who you're becoming, and the more emotional you can get about it, the faster you will become it.

6. GET OUT YOUR CREDIT CARD AND PAY FOR SOME HELP ALREADY

Getting some coaching or mentoring is perhaps the fastest and best thing you can do to make a massive change in the shortest amount of time. I'm not, and I kind of am, just saying this because I'm a coach and have watched my clients do the impossible. I'm also saying it because I've *been* coached within an inch of my life and know how radically it's changed my world. Think about it—professional athletes work with coaches their entire careers. They don't decide all of a sudden, *alrighty, I just made eight million bucks hitting a ball around this year. I think I'm pretty well set to do this on my own*. They continue to get coaching so they can stay at their peak level and keep growing. What makes you think you think you can do it all by yourself (especially if you've

7. GET YOUR BODY IN ON IT

Your mind will follow where your body leads. If you're in a bad mood and remember to stand up nice and tall and straight, your mood will automatically lift. And when you're in shape and have tons of energy, you feel like you can take over the world. If you're serious about getting your act together, stop being a lazy cow. Get the blood flowing, eat food that excites you *and* nourishes you, get your breathing deeper. Use your mind, body, and soul together to make this thing happen for yourself.

ADVANCED BODY OPTION: Okay, so this is totally weird and won't go over well, but I'm going to give it to you anyway because it works. If you want to really get yourself rock solid and determined and pumped up, pound your chest and punch your fists in the air while you repeat your affirmations at the same time. Yell things like, "I am powerful, I am confident, The Universe has my back, and I am going to kick ass!" Or whatever your deal is in the affirmations department. Get your body engaged and anchor in the words physically and your affirmations will have far greater power. The mind and the body are way more powerful together than either one is alone.

8. USE YOUR SECRET WEAPONS

Make a playlist of songs that gets you pumped up, listen to motivational tapes, surround yourself with pictures of people who think you're awesome, wear clothes that make you feel sexy and smart, dance, scream, pound your chest, go for a run while listening to the theme from *Rocky*—figure out what makes you feel like you could carry a horse over your head and do it as often as possible. You are going for the gold here, you have to stay in The Zone.

9. LOVE YOURSELF

With a kung fu grip.

CHAPTER 27:

BEAM ME UP, SCOTTY

Nothing is impossible, the word itself says "I'm possible."
—**Audrey Hepburn; actress, icon, fabulist**

My grandmother on my mother's side lived to be one hundred years old. Nana was as WASPy as they make 'em: prissy, reserved, able to avoid confrontation with the skilled precision of an F-16 pilot. For as long as I can remember, she always looked exactly the same. She was eternally adorned in a cardigan, pinned together at the top by an antique broach, her pink lipstick and sparkly brown eyes shining through a face-full of wrinkles that erupted in a series of "oh dears" every time she laughed.

In her long lifetime, Nana witnessed the birthing of such pivotal human achievements as the phone, the car, the TV, human flight, the computer, the internet and rock and roll.

The two things that blew her mind the most, however, were putting a man on the moon and the soda dispensers at McDonalds. She'd stand there watching, gripped by disbelief, as an employee placed a cup, small, medium or large, beneath a spout, pushed a button and walked away, leaving the machine to fill it up the perfect, proper amount. "How does it know where to stop?" Nana would shake her head, mortified, "How does it *know*?!"

After we figured out how to clone a sheep, she pretty much threw in the towel on ever questioning anything again.

One day my family took her out for lunch to a restaurant on the top floor of some giant hotel. When we got into the elevator, someone accidentally pushed the button for the floor we were already on the moment the doors closed, making them open right back up again. Thinking we'd just gone up forty-five-flights in a split second, we watched my sweet little grandmother exit the elevator, nervously patting her hair as she wandered down the hallway muttering to herself, "Why not?"

I want to sign off here by encouraging you to pursue your dreams with the same belief that anything is possible as a little old lady in knee-high stockings and sensible heels who was born in 1903 and lived through the most technologically flabbergasting century to date.

Whatever you desire to do with your precious life—write jokes or rock out or start a business or learn to speak Greek or quit your job or raise a bunch of kids or fall in love or lose your flab or open orphanages around the world or direct movies or save dolphins or make millions or live in a canyon in a loincloth—believe that it's possible. And that it's available to you. And that you deserve to be/do/have it.

Why not?

Give yourself the permission and the means (yes, this includes the money), to be who you are REGARDLESS OF WHAT ANYBODY ELSE THINKS OR BELIEVES IS POSSIBLE. Do not deny yourself the life you want to live because you're worried you're not good enough or that you'll be judged or that it's too risky, because who does that benefit? No one, that's who. When you live your life doing the things that turn you on, that you're good at, that bring you joy, that make you shove stuff in people's faces and scream, "check this out!!!" you walk around so lit up that you shoot sunbeams out of yer eyeballs. Which automatically lights up the world around you. Which is precisely why you are here: to shine your big-ass ball of fire onto this world of ours. A world that literally depends upon light to survive.

You are powerful. You are loved. You are surrounded by miracles.

Believe, *really* believe that what you desire is here and available to you. And you can have it all.

Love Yourself

You are a badass.

RESOURCES

Below is a list of some of the books I read and teachers I studied with while honing my own badassery. And while these are some of my all-time favorites (that I strongly suggest you check out), my list is constantly growing and evolving, so if you'd like more all-inclusive and up-to-date suggestions, please sign up at www.JenSincero.com and I shall keep you abreast.

BOOKS

Ask and It is Given: Learning to Manifest Your Desires *by Esther and Jerry Hicks*

This is an excellent starter book. Well-written and not hellishly long, it talks all about the Law of Attraction in depth and how to manifest what you want into your life. The Freak Factor is super high: co-author Esther Hicks was your average housewife until she suddenly started channeling this spirit named Abraham. The book, and all her work, contains the teachings of this dude Abraham, whoever the hell he is/was, but his information is good AND Esther is pretty entertaining in her live recordings, although the book is more straightforward. First half is teachings; second half is to-do's.

The Four Agreements: A Practical Guide to Personal Freedom *by Don Miguel Ruiz*

Good, short, based on the wisdom passed down from the author's Toltec ancestors. Basically, it talks about the four things you need to do to live an awesome life: be impeccable with your word, don't take anything personally, don't make assumptions, and always do your best. It's worth a read for sure as it lays out some very simple and profound truths that will absolutely change your life for the better if you live by them. And it looks really good on your coffee table.

The Game of Life and How to Play It *by Florence Scovel Shinn*

This book constantly refers to The Bible and Jesus, but it's easy to love whether or not you're religious because it's crammed full of valuable spiritual lessons and lots and lots of old-timey stories. The writing is real pedestrian and very grandmotherly, but I love the simplicity and how well the stories illustrate what she's talking about. It's short, to the point, and blunt, much like sitting down with an old lady who wants to give you a talking to about the way things are around here.

The Power of Now: A Guide to Spiritual Enlightenment *by Eckhart Tolle*

If you're new to the whole Ego (or Big Snooze) thing and really want to grasp the transformative nature of being present, this is basically The Bible. It challenges you to see the world in a different way and does a great job of at helping you grasp some pretty deep theories about reality and time and perspective. This is another one where the Freak Factor is very high: Eckhart was suicidal, all ready to do himself in and then woke up one morning all enlightened and transformed and was in such a state of bliss that he spent the next two years sitting on a park bench, playing with his lip (I'm not kidding). Then he channeled this book.

As a Man Thinketh *by James Allen*

This is, shockingly all about the mighty mind and how to use it to master your world. Considering the fact that if you can really truly get that skill down, you can create the most awesome life ever, reading this book, over and over and over until it becomes second nature is time well spent. It's another old-timey one written back in ye olde day, but it's still extremely quotable and relevant today.

The Creative Habit: Learn It and Use It For Life *by Twyla Tharp*

Written by no-nonsense, world-renowned dance choreographer Twyla Tharp, this is one of the best spankings I ever got in the old get-your-act-together department. As the title suggests, it's all about creating good habits, which, if you do nothing else, will completely change your life for the better. Full of stories and tips and whip cracking, this is one of my favorites. 'Cuz she kind of scares me.

Losing My Virginity: How I've Survived, Had Fun and Made a Fortune Doing Business My Way *by Richard Branson*

This is an awesome read—I devoured the whole thing in one sitting. Richard Branson, founder of Virgin Records and Virgin Airlines, is a maniac and one of the most inspiring people on two legs as far as I'm concerned. The book details his life from when he started his little record shop to becoming one of the most famous and radical entrepreneurs who went on to buy his own island and fly hot air balloons over the ocean in the jet stream. I would like very much to party with this guy.

IMPORTANT BIOGRAPHY NOTE: I've listed Richard Branson's biography because it's one of my favorites, but pretty much any biography/autobiography about the people you personally find inspiring is totally worth reading. I could list about seventy more here, but you may not find the life and accomplishments of, say, Dolly Parton or Eleanor Roosevelt, as riveting and inspiring as I do. I strongly suggest you actually take the time to read books about the people who light you up, because it's one of the best ways to get inspired to change your life.

Practical Intuition *by Laura Day*

Long hailed as a leading master of intuition, Laura Day has worked with everyone from high-powered business people to hippies to celebrities to financial analysts to housewives. She is the queen of showing people how to access their intuition so they can make more informed decisions and design more authentic lives. This book gives all her secrets and tried and true tips on connecting with your inner GPS via exercises and case studies.

The Seven Spiritual Laws of Success: A Practical Guide to the Fulfillment of Your Dreams *by Deepak Chopra*

I'm a huge fan of not having to read too much to get the information I want, and of knowing how much I'm gonna have to do ahead of time to get where I want to go. Good old Deepak breaks achieving success down into seven, easy-to-follow steps based on spiritual principles. This is one of my all-time favorites for its small size and profoundly potent advice. It delivers deeply spiritual and powerful information in bite-sized chunks and gives clear exercises on using it in your everyday life to achieve what you want.

You Can Heal Your Life *by Louise Hay*

Louise Hay is a modern day self-help pioneer who cured herself of cancer using her highly-lauded principles of self-love and who now has her own empire with a publishing company and everything. This book is one of my faves, even though it's SUPER woo-woo, full of affirmations and general gooeyness, but in the ever-critical self-love department, it doesn't get any better than this. The back of the book is all about the body and how all our injuries and dis-eases can be traced back to negative thought patterns. So if you break your leg, you can look it up and see that it's because you're scared of moving forward (or something, don't quote me on that) and get an affirmation from Louise on how to heal yourself. I have a friend who completely cured himself of something the doctors were baffled by through reading this book and doing what it says.

Creating Money: Keys To Abundance *by Sanaya Roman and Duane Packer*

The title of this book is a tad misleading because it's about so much more than money, yet since most people want to make more money, the good news is they'll pick it up and get way more than they bargained for by reading it and doing what it says. While it does indeed teach you how to create money, it also gives clear instruction on meditation, clearing blocks, manifesting, working with energy, gaining clarity, etc. All of which contribute to manifesting money, as well as pretty much everything else, into your life. Easy to read and follow with simple exercises and deceptively deep concepts broken down, this is an awesome starter book as well as one to always have around to provide important reminders and re-alignment.

The Science Of Getting Rich *by Wallace D. Wattles*

The very first sentence of this book made me slam it shut and leave it untouched for years. It reads: "Whatever may be said in praise of poverty, the fact remains that it is not possible to live a really complete or successful life unless one is rich." Hello? How gross is that?! It offended me to my hippie core, until I understood what it was really saying and that, erm, you kind of can't —not if you want to fully express yourself, anyway. "Rich" simply means that you have everything you need to share your gifts fully with the world and stay at the highest vibration while you do it, whatever that looks like for you. This is now easily the book I recommend to people the most, and the one I read over and over. But you have to let a lot go because it will absolutely go up your nose if you're still working on your issues around it being okay to make money.

Think and Grow Rich *by Napoleon Hill*

This is the other contender for the "Best Wealth Consciousness Book Ever," and another old-timey one. I forgot to mention that Wallace Wattle's book is old-timey, too, but hello, look at the guy's name. Anyway, Napoleon Hill interviewed the most successful businessmen at the time to gather the information for this incredible, how-to guide. I read this book over and over, too. It's very to the point, a total ass-kicker, and breaks everything down into simple, easy-to-follow instructions. Do what he says (and really do all of it) and you will be large and in charge.

Finding Your Own North Star: Claiming the Life You Were Meant to Live *by Martha Beck*

I've seen Martha speak and have read lots of her work and really love her voice—so refreshing and brilliant and hilarious. This book is awesome, really walks you through some good steps and asks some great questions to get you the clarity you seek. She's big on looking past just what's going on in your head and connecting with your body to get clarity and guidance from there as well. She's had a super successful coaching institute for ages and is one of my favorites in the field.

Getting to I Do: The Secret to Doing Relationships Right *by Dr. Patricia Allen*

I'm pretty sure I tore the cover off this one before carrying it around, but in spite of its totally unforgivable title, there are some real eye-openers in here about the nature of men and women and how differently we go about relationships. Written for women by someone who has coached thousands of happy couples into long-term relationships, it's full of brilliant insights and tips on how to find and be in the relationship of your dreams. As with all this stuff, there will probably be parts you don't agree with (she's like a strict Christian mother on the sex issue), but it's got lots of very valuable information and is definitely worth a read by both men and women.

Loving What Is: Four Questions That Can Change Your Life *by Byron Katie*

Read this book! I demand it. It is the Holy Grail of being happy in your relationships. Based on what Katie calls "The Work"—which is essentially just asking yourself four simple, yet profound, questions—this book spends about ten pages walking you through the steps of The Work and a couple hundred on case studies. It's basically like watching Katie perform her magic on all sorts of people, from those who've been brutally raped to people who've lost their children to those who want happier marriages. She walks them through her process and they suddenly find peace and freedom. It's so cool AND The Work is a piece of cake. When you read it, I recommend reading the case studies first and then doing The Work on yourself instead of the other way around. Seeing her do it over and over will make it much easier for you to get better results when you try it on yourself.

The Way of the Superior Man: A Spiritual Guide to Mastering the Challenges of Women, Work and Sexual Desire *by David Deida*

This book is made for a man, but the ladies must read it, too, if they really want to understand how men work. I thought it was brilliant and fascinating and explained SO much about the opposite sex that made me respect men even more. And the guys I've suggested it to said it was massively empowering. It speaks to, and explains, the highest version of masculinity, reminding us ladies why we love the fellas so much and reminding men how truly awesome they are/can be.

SEMINARS

PAX—Allison Armstrong

I took one of their brilliant seminars for women called "Understanding Men, Celebrating Women," all about the difference between the sexes that had me on the floor—how did I make it this far and not know any of this? I thought it was so well done and not even that cheesy. I went to just that one seminar but I highly enjoyed their recordings as well and have heard great things about their other workshops.

The Hoffman Institute

Kay, so, this is the full-on, *are-you-fucking-kidding-me* one. This involves beating pillows with baseball bats while shrieking at the top of your lungs, marrying yourself, singing lullabies to your inner child—basically everything that would have most people running for their lives. It was so over the top that you couldn't help but give into it because what the hell else could you do? Luckily, it's run by incredibly sweet and skilled people who also have excellent senses of humor about what they're asking you to do and you spend a solid week of nonstop seminar and digging deep into your past and your limiting beliefs and letting them go. It's like a limiting-belief high-colonic. I loved it as much as I hated it and highly, highly recommend it. Brilliant and transformative (and the food was awesome).

Other good speakers to keep an eye out for: Martha Beck, Esther Hicks, Marianne Williamson, Byron Katie, Wayne Dyer, David Neagle, Deepak Chopra, Gabrielle Bernstien.

ACKNOWLEDGMENTS

Thanks to everyone at the funny farm, especially Horseface McGee and Goatly Thing One and Goatly Thing Two for keeping me company, staring at me while I wrote, cracking me up, and showing me that I'm capable of unconditional love by chewing through the door and pooping all over the couch. I owe many thanks to my agent, Peter Steinberg, for all his hard work, support and camaraderie. Gigantic, tearful, are-you-kidding-me's go to Gina DeVee for saving the day with her insight, humor and ruthlessly loving red pen, and to Alice Fiori and Bill Campbell for their friendship, endless generosity, support and high thread count sheets. Thanks to Jennifer Kasius, Monica Parcell and everyone at Running Press, Anders Pederson, Crystalyn Hoffman, Julie Faherty, my sweet mama, Michael Flowers, Katharine Dever, and The Universe, for all the endless awesomeness.

From Byron, Austen and Darwin

to some of the most acclaimed and original
contemporary writing, John Murray takes pride in
bringing you powerful, prizewinning, absorbing
and provocative books that will entertain you
today and become the classics of tomorrow.

We put a lot of time and passion into what we
publish and how we publish it, and we'd like to
hear what you think.

Be part of John Murray – share your views with us at:

www.johnmurray.co.uk

 johnmurraybooks

 @johnmurrays

 johnmurraybooks